Praise for Bead by Bead

Bead by Bead is not just a benign book about ... frolicking journey through the history and use ... Suzanne Henley does not stop there. As South... reluctant prayer warrior, she invites us to walk ... aglow with the shimmering beads of the Holy S|

—Sybil MacBeth, author of *Praying in Color:*
Drawing a New Path to God and other books

This book is a work of spiritual art and alchemy—brilliant wordsmith meets creative soul! Makes me want to grab a set of prayer beads and allow my life to be enriched and transformed, word by word, bead by bead.

—Linda Douty, author of *Rhythms of Growth:*
365 Meditations to Nurture the Soul

With insight, passion, and wit, Henley shows us how to hold our prayers in our hands as well as our heart.

—Richard Rohr, author of *Falling Backwards* and *Immortal Diamond*

What a beautiful exploration of hurt and heart, love and loss, gratitude and thanksgiving, all within the fascinating framework of Protestant prayer beads. Suzanne Henley has penned a unique collection of stories that provide healing and hope for anyone navigating the tumultuous twists and turns of life. In other words, this is a book for everyone.

—Julie Cantrell, *New York Times* and *USA TODAY*
bestselling author of *Perennials*

In *Bead by Bead* the Holy Spirit rides a Harley, God arrives with the tapping of goat hooves, and Jesus ambles in as Clyde the Carpenter. Henley's delightful book invites us to use a simple—or metaphorical—string of beads to fall in love with the wonder of life.

—Ellen Morris Prewitt, author of *Making Crosses:*
A Creative Connection to God

...nley is fresh, illuminating, and wise, singing her journey as a gift for any ...ker.

—Br. Timothy Jolley, OHC, former prior, Holy Cross Monastery, West Park, New York, Founder of Mariya uMama weThemba (Mary, Mother of Hope) Monastery, Grahamstown, South Africa

A lifelong struggler with prayer, constantly seeking but rarely finding the elusive sweet spot of prayer I have always imagined to exist, I found this fresh new book to be filled with joy and hope. A how-to manual in part, *Bead by Bead* is infinitely more. Suzanne Henley's keen intuition and insight, often delivered with quirky, laugh-out-loud humor, touched my heart unexpectedly. Never preachy and always with great humanity, her willingness to share details of her own journey, with a light but deeply affecting touch, lifts this book from the ordinary. It's a gem.

—The Rev. Buddy Stallings, Retired Rector, St. Bartholomew's, New York City

SUZANNE HENLEY

Mary Edith ~ many years! Suzanne

bead
by
bead

The Ancient Way
of Praying Made New

PARACLETE PRESS
BREWSTER, MASSACHUSETTS

2018
First Printing

Bead by Bead: The Ancient Way of Praying Made New

© 2018 by
Suzanne Henley

ISBN
978-1-61261-918-7

The Paraclete Press name and logo (dove on cross) are trademarks of Paraclete Press, Inc.

10 9 8 7 6 5 4 3 2 1

Library of Congress
Cataloging-in-Publication Data

Names: Henley, Suzanne, author.
Title: Bead by bead : the ancient way of praying made new / Suzanne Henley.
Description: Brewster, MA : Paraclete Press, Inc., 2018.
Identifiers: LCCN 2017057486 | ISBN 9781612619187 (trade paper)
Subjects: LCSH: Beads--Religious aspects--Christianity. | Prayer--Christianity.
Classification: LCC BV215 .H485 2018 | DDC 248.3/2--dc23
LC record available at https://lccn.loc.gov/2017057486

Published by
Paraclete Press
Brewster, Massachusetts
www.paracletepress.com

Printed in the United States of America

For Momma, Daddy, and Jeff;

for my children and grandchildren—

Blair, Noel, Kate, and Otto; Sarah and Brad;

Bailey, Walker, Charles, and Hollan; and Walter and Katie;

and for Jim Cole, the prince of my dotage

Prayer is dangerous
and the entrance way to wholeness.

—PHYLLIS TICKLE, *Prayer Is a Place*

❦

The Mystery in anyone may speak to them and heal them in the grocery store. It may speak to us and heal us too. Knowing this enables us to listen to life from the place in us that is Mystery also. Mystery requires that we relinquish an endless search for answers and become willing to not understand. . . . Perhaps real wisdom lies in not seeking answers at all. Any answer we find will not be true for long. An answer is a place where we can fall asleep as life moves past us to its next question. After all these years I have begun to wonder if the secret of living well is not in having all the answers but in pursuing unanswerable questions in good company.

—RACHEL NAOMI REMEN, *My Grandfather's Blessings*

Contents

Rebranding Prayer:
The House Guests

*I think we are well advised to keep on nodding terms with
the people we used to be, whether we find them attractive
company or not. Otherwise they turn up unannounced and
surprise us, come hammering on the mind's door at 4 a.m.
of a bad night and demand to know who deserted them,
who betrayed them, who is going to make amends.*

—Joan Didion, *Slouching Toward Bethlehem*

This book began as a simple, straightforward primer about the ancient history of prayer beads. Instructions for making them and traditional and modern prayer suggestions would close out the chapters. *An easy one, two, three,* I thought.

Work on the book seemed to be going as expected—methodical, predictable—until the writing decided to take on a life of its own. Loud, uninvited squatters began showing up at all hours at my imagination's front door, disturbing the neighbors, blocking driveways, and making demands.

These gremlins of my mind—sometimes unwashed and ill-groomed, some dragging Linus blankets, some with eyelash extensions and pouty lips—moved in with their heavy baggage, stacks of old *New Yorker*s, bad breath, and loud voices. They did not knock. They just pushed in, plopped down their backpacks, and set up house with their egos. They waved their cigars, passed gas, and made pronouncements.

"People don't just sit around all day with prayer beads in their hands waiting for the Holy Spirit to ride up on a Harley, Sweetheart. We want some action!"

And they persisted. So I created some examples of day-to-day, quick activities readers could use to close themselves off from the wrought busyness of the day and pray even when they are without their beads, momentarily erasing the everyday to connect with the timeless. Some examples border on silliness, simply to underscore that praying is fair game anywhere.

But my squatters weren't satisfied: "Yeah, we like the Desert Fathers and Mothers, and Lady Godiva's prayer bead legacy is a good read, and we're glad you included Thomas Merton, but we still want more. We want stories!" One of my squatters—flicking his cigar ashes onto the carpet—announced, "Rebranding! That's what prayer needs. That's what you need to do! *Rebrand* prayer. It's gotten a bad rap."

So, because I'm from the South—it is not just a cliché that Southerners like to tell stories—and because, as William Faulkner reminded us, the past is never dead; we are all stories and tote the history of their imprinted baggage throughout our lives—the book gradually grew to include a few personal narratives I now recognize as experiences—some perhaps unorthodox—of prayer.

Other than liturgy recited at church and a lifetime of blessings at meals, I am a latecomer to serious prayer. I am by no means a prayer warrior, and I'm never even quite sure whom or what I think I am talking to. I seem to fling random, unscheduled thoughts into the universe assuming they're being caught by a God very, very good at playing outfield, a Willy Mays of prayer.

I have no idea whether prayer produces any external results. I have come to believe, though, if nothing else, it is where I most squarely meet myself. I think it is the psychic glue between my conscious and shadow self where we all wrestle with Jacob's angel and count our scars later. It is where we ask, sometimes with fury, sometimes with a whimper, for strength and courage when surrounded by incomprehensible tragedy and unmitigated grief. It is where, sometimes crying "uncle," tightly wadding the pillowcase into a tear-limp ball, and other times with childlike wonder, we gasp, "Thank you." I have found prayer to be a safari tracking down the wild beasts of my thoughts in tall grass. It is also an adventure like scratching off the boxes on a lottery ticket. It reveals who we are to ourselves. And that's where God often seems to set up shop. Each prayer, when genuine, is a birth, a labored delivery of twins: both a new self and a new face of God.

Praying is not just an arcane, dusty practice that a group of humorless, self-righteous old men sat down and made up a long time ago. It is not just words in a prayer book. It's not a milquetoast, rehearsed exhortation delivered in a faux-devout voice to begin a citywide prayer breakfast with cold scrambled eggs. We carry this need for connection in our guts, whether at the time we recognize these experiences—often mundane, unbidden, off-the-wall—as prayer or not. The need is in the DNA of the pulsing molecules we now know we all share. And it should grab us at the core of our beings.

Acts of prayer can happen in the produce section of the grocery store, in the middle of a fishing stream, in a darkened psychiatric unit, in the Large Hadron Collider at CERN. Just as swaying full-body to a gospel hymn that raises you out of yourself in a church pew is prayer, so too dancing on a whim by yourself in your pajamas across the kitchen floor to John Lee Hooker's "Boom Boom" at top volume can also be prayer. It is the combination of repetitive muscle memory and inner spirit gone a'courting, a date with the mystery in which "we live and move and have our being."

"Oh, yuck, don't be silly! And quit preaching!" the rowdy house guests shrilled in unison in my ear. "Just let the stories do the telling."

The stories I've included stand as stepping stones at various points in my life, each story a prayer bead in my life's rosary, where, like circling a set of prayer beads from start to finish, I've learned to celebrate the paradox that "in the beginning is my end" and "in my end is my beginning."

The book is also an adult version of Show and Tell of some of the hundreds and hundreds of sets of prayer beads I have made—each unique, many commissioned to be carried to diverse people around the world. Many of the stories I tell are accounts of these real people for whom praying bead by bead has become an essential spiritual practice.

I have learned that prayers do not need semicolons, and the Holy Spirit doesn't need a Harley. Each breath we breathe, in and out, *is* the Holy Spirit, the holy *pneuma*. Each breath itself is prayer; each of us, our own set of prayer beads. We get to carry this abundance with us, step by step. May the thanks I give also be abundant, towing anointed gremlins in the dust of my wake.

Prologue

It is dawn. I sit with a cup of English breakfast tea at my work space, a salvaged farm table marked by the hieroglyphs of many years' use. My quiet studio on the second floor is a tree-house perch among giant oaks pressing against the two walls of windows. The early light snakes through the leaves and creates moving prisms in the 100-year-old bubbled-glass panes.

Stacks of clear plastic bins, hundreds of beads full, bank the walls behind me, the bin drawers pulled out at haphazard levels, miscellaneous strands of ancient beads spilling over the sides. Mounds of various beads on the table wait patiently. In the growing light the room becomes a messy swirl of color.

I pick up a handful of my favorite Mongolian sand beads from the Gobi Desert—translucent and wind-pitted and older than we can imagine—and some beads of ancient Roman glass fragments from the Afghan Silk Road. I press them, rough and irregularly shaped, deep into the meat of my palm.

I think of those who spent their lives thousands of years ago chiseling our earth's core for shards that would become these beads—our universe's first art form; of those who hunkered, precariously bow-drilling holes in them; and of those who painstakingly polished by hand, sometimes for a month each, the roughed shards into a smooth bead. I imagine a connection from the tendons of my hands to theirs, to their sweat, their lean muscles, their dirty fingernails. I think of what these artisans traded their labor for and of the merchants who traveled on camel, by foot, and by ship, sailing the continents through rough seas and parched deserts across centuries and cultures.

I think of the path of a single bead from the wrist of a Buddhist monk, next to the heart of an Asian princess, traded by a Bedouin shepherd for a chicken, tossed in the waves of a ship carrying it from Venice to Nigeria, passed with its history from calloused hand to calloused hand to my own. I feel a connection to the volcanic gifts and shifting tectonic plates of our young, spinning universe; to those earliest peoples who first felt the need to hold these beads as rosaries or malas; and to those who through the years have worn down their rough edges in repetitions of supplication, fear, gratitude, duty, and awe.

I am the latest in a long line to add the imprint of my hands' oils to the human- and earth-marked patina of all those who have come before me. I feel the weight of their histories in my palm.

And, with a final glance of thanksgiving through the morning windows, I take off my slippers, as Moses was told to do on holy ground, and bow my head toward my table to begin creating another set of prayer beads, beads that soon will come to bear the patina of its next recipient's longing and joy.

In the Beginning

"You look like a deer in the headlights," my friend Robbie laughed. "Or maybe like you've just seen a snake handler." It was 2005 and Robbie, in charge at the time of Adult Formation at Holy Communion Episcopal Church in Memphis, asked me to make three sets of Episcopal prayer beads for her upcoming class on prayer.

I was appalled. An Episcopalian, I had been a Southern Baptist as a child, but neither of these denominations prepared me for the thought of rosaries with a bleeding Christ affixed. I did not know a modern animal called Episcopal or Anglican prayer beads even existed.

Robbie knew I had some beads because I did commissions in fused glass—wall sculptures, kitchen and bath tiles, drawer pulls, jewelry, mosaic murals—in which I often incorporated beads on wire. She emailed me a diagram for the prayer beads and, with a wince, I agreed to make three simple examples.

Then someone who'd seen them asked me to make her a set. And then another, and then another. Always staying true to the basic design, over the next several years I began to experiment with combinations of colors and textures and increasingly incorporated handmade, antique beads.

Someone asked me to turn hers into a necklace. I balked. I did not want to interrupt the line of prayer with a commercial clasp but realized I could add extra beads at the apex (I used to think of them as Southern Baptist Spontaneous Prayer Beads) so that they would slip over someone's head without interruption.

Now, unless someone specifically says he or she wants only Christian elements—increasingly rare I have noted—I also incorporate antique, handmade Buddhist, Hindu, and Islamic prayer beads as well as rare Hebron beads of Dead Sea salt. I use replicas of third-century Ethiopian Coptic crosses and Stars of David, hand-carved Chinese jade pendants, or river rocks collected from my fishing sites. I sell them but do not actively market them, and I include a card describing the provenance of the beads with each set.

I have made more than eight hundred sets of prayer beads but have never duplicated. I want each recipient to receive a gift that is the same basic design but unique, just as each of us is. People have commissioned them to take to the Dalai Lama, Pope Francis, bishops and priests in Uruguay, sherpas in Nepal and Tibet, Chinese artist-activist Ai Weiwei, a Chinese iman and shaman, a Thai elephant mahout, a monk in Ethiopia, and to many who are terminally ill.

The beads are a visual and physical reminder to pray without ceasing. They are the conduit to a connection of mind and body and spirit seeking union with the great Mystery. Creating these sets is in itself a quiet form of meditative prayer for me, a combined aesthetic and spiritual experience in which the boundaries of space and time disappear.

Although my beads have been carried to remote places and interesting people, none have seemed more startlingly exotic than an experience I had with them in my own home.

Pierre occasionally worked in my yard and was a member of my construction crew, but one day yard work morphed into housework. "You know, Miss Suzanne, I learned housekeeping—dusting, ironing, mopping—from the nuns when I worked at St. Joseph's Hospital. They'd come along after me and do the white glove test."

"That's great about your skills, Pierre, but don't call me 'Miss Suzanne.' We're not on a plantation anymore. You make me feel like Scarlett."

"Yes, m'am."

"No 'm'am.' Just 'yes' or 'ok.' Ok?"

"Yes, m'am. Damn. I mean 'ok.'"

He ironed beautifully.

One of his regular chores once a week was one my knees hated: crawling, literally, around my studio floor picking up all the beads that had rolled off my worktable while making prayer beads. I'm a messy worker, about as far down the scale from OCD as one can get, but Pierre methodically picked up bead after bead and sorted them. He became very familiar with all the drawers and pots of bead collections and paraphernalia I used in making prayer beads.

One day when he came to work, he said, "Would you make me a prayer bead necklace instead of paying me?" And then he picked up a replica of a third-century Ethiopian Star of David off the table and handed it to me. "And I want this on it instead of a cross."

Although I thought it curious he'd want a prayer necklace and found his choice of a Star of David a bit strange—he'd grown up in a Southern black gospel church rather than a synagogue—I said, "Sure," without questioning.

Every time I saw him that summer, he had on a white, sleeveless tee shirt—his dark, slim arms flexing with muscle definition and the bright red coral beads of his prayer necklace both highlighted against the white of his tee shirt.

One day about a month after I'd made his necklace, he arrived and began a conversation without preamble. "I have a deal for you, Suzanne. I want you to make as many of these necklaces as you can for me." Obviously I was curious. "I can sell as many as you can make; you can charge whatever you want to. You'll get paid with cash straight out of the safe. You can make a ton of money." He was almost breathless he was so excited.

I just stared at him. "They're for my guys," he said. "Everyone wants one." He held up the Star of David. "This is our symbol. It's the symbol of the Gangster Disciples. There're about forty thousand of us. You know in my 'hood I'm called O.G. Pierre, Original Gangster Pierre. Each one of the six points of the star has a meaning: love, life, loyalty, knowledge, wisdom, and understanding."

He makes the gang sound like they're a Brownie troop in a Methodist basement, I thought.

"You can make a ton of money," he repeated. "You'll be famous!"

I just stared. It took a few seconds to process this scene. I was simultaneously horrified and intrigued by the image of becoming the little old white-haired lady who made prayer bead necklaces for one of the oldest, largest, and most dangerous African American gangs in the country.

I wondered if I could include the distinction in my obituary.

True to the Southern way, I didn't want to appear rude to Pierre and told him I needed to think about the proposition. I know I've made Jesus's hair stand on end several times in my life, but this possibility was probably a contender for first place. I could imagine his toenails curling. And I could see the next day's headline: "Episcopal Vestry Member Arrested on Gang Charges."

The next day I said no to Pierre.

I don't know if anyone else in the universe has ever had this same experience, but it is a highlight of Unintended Consequences in my life with prayer beads.

PRAYER BEADS FOR SOPHIE

Kazakhstani picture jasper; hand-carved Chinese jade; silver-capped Tibetan turquoise; Indian Ocean chank shell, sacred to Hindu and Buddhists; a hand-etched bone Islamic prayer bead; an antique, handmade Ethiopian telsum protective prayer amulet with Tibetan carnelians; an ancient Hebron bead of Dead Sea salt; a Kenyan batik mudcloth bone bead; 200 BCE fragments of Roman glass excavated at the site of the statues of Buddha blown up by the Taliban on the Afghan Silk Road; ancient, naturally formed Mongolian Gobi Desert sand; an antique, handmade silver Islamic prayer bead; a matte-frosted Tibetan banded agate; and a replica of a third-century Ethiopian Coptic cross.

May the irregularities of these beads remind you to gently embrace our imperfections; may their roughness be smoothed by the prayers of your hands; and, reflecting on the many hands through which these beads have been passed to you across generations and cultures, may you be reminded we are all held in the hands of the same God. May you move through your day knowing you are wreathed in prayer. We are one.

Episcopal in design, these beads invite the prayers of any spiritual tradition.
This is a one-of-a-kind creation.
shenlely@bellsouth.net

1
Talking to God in Braille

A fascinating, if unexpected, 130,000-year-old path leads from excavations of a cave in Croatia to the annual international Godiva Chocolate Miss Lady Godiva contest. It is a winding course from Southeastern Europe to South Africa to Israel to China to the Himalayas, across the Egyptian desert to Rome and the court of Henry VIII, then from Telephone, Texas, to New York and beyond. The path is spiritual as well as geographic: It traces the evolution and history of Hindu, Buddhist, Islamic, Jewish, Roman Catholic, and Protestant prayer beads.

A Presbyterian or a Baptist in Omaha very possibly does not care—and perhaps is relieved—that he's not one of the almost four billion people who owns a set of prayer beads. Ears might perk up, however, to hear that since 1987—contrary to the decades-long decrease in worldwide mainline church affiliation we hear about so often—Protestant prayer beads are being created, bought, and used increasingly by Presbyterians, Methodists, Baptists, Episcopalians, Lutherans, and Unitarians—and by the neighbor down the street who is Wiccan.

Googling the term "prayer beads" online in the fall of 2016 brought up 4,400,000 entries; seven months later, that figure had risen to more than 7,700,000 sites. The term "rosary" produced 29,200,000 results, which six months later had grown to more than 34,000,000 entries. YouTube offers hundreds of videos demonstrating how to make sets of beads. Even videos directed at making Pagan beads show hundreds of choices.

It is indeed noteworthy that the gift for each of the 864 international delegates to the 2016 General Conference of the United Methodist Church was a set of prayer beads. Although membership in bricks-and-mortar denominational worship is declining, the increase in the use of prayer beads illuminates a cultural phenomenon: People are not abandoning worship; many are simply carrying their altars with them in their pockets.

The word *bead* is derived from the mid-fourteenth-century Old English *bede* (prayer bead) and the German cognate *bitte* (please). *To bid one's beads* means to count or pray one's beads. All religions' prayer beads denote the practice of connecting body and spirit in counting prayers. "To use beads with a prayer, Indian or Moslem or Christian," says Madeline L'Engle, "is to enflesh the words, make thought tangible."

Before looking at the history of Christian, and specifically Protestant, prayer beads, we must first briefly consider several of the world's other religions, all of which use prayer beads as a means both of keeping count of the number of prayers prayed and of connecting the physical body with the divine.

Hinduism, a fusion of earlier Indian traditions originating between 500 and 300 BCE, is the world's oldest existing and third largest religion, practiced by more than one billion people. A recently discovered statue of the god Vishnu in Vietnam is dated to four thousand years ago, however, and the earliest known use of prayer beads is a third-century BCE Indian statue of a Hindu holy man draped in them. Although beads known as *sha sha* were used with spiritual connotations in Egypt in 3200 BCE, the first scholarly authenticated instructions for the use of prayer beads is in Hinduism's *Arthava Veda*, written around 800 BCE.

Beads are typically used so one can focus on the meaning or sound of a mantra, which is often repeated hundreds or even thousands of times. The Chinese abacus is possibly the source of the idea behind the creation of the counting beads called a *mala* ("rose" or "garland" in Sanskrit). A Hindu set of beads is usually composed of 108 seeds—*rudraksha* ("Shiva's eyes") seeds for followers of Shiva, *tulsi* or basil for followers of Vishnu. Both gods are aspects of Brahma, creator of all, and each of the mala's 108 beads stands for one of Brahma's 108 names. *Namajapa* is the recitation of all Brahma's names.

Buddhism—derived from *budhi*, "to awaken," and referring to the awakening of Siddhartha Gautama, known as the Buddha—evolved out of Hinduism in India around 2,500 years ago. It also uses a mala of usually 108 beads, but for reasons different from those of Hinduism.

The 108 beads refer to the number of passions one is trying to end. Shorter malas can also be made of 18, 27, or 54 beads. Some Tibetan Buddhists use malas called *Trengwa* ("the purring of cats") of 21 or 28 beads. The mantra used is the well-known *Om mani padme hum*, very roughly translated as "The jewel of the heart of the lotus," considered the true words of the Buddha. One set of Japanese Buddhist prayer beads can help the user count up to 36,736 prayers!

Judaism, the oldest of monotheistic religions, is the only world religion without a specific use of prayer beads, a custom some Hebrew scholars consider "pagan." The four-cornered, fringed prayer shawl, the *tallit*, worn by men and sometimes by women for Shabbat and High Holy Days, however, is in fact a form of counting prayers. In Numbers 15:38–40, God instructs Moses:

> Speak to the Israelites, and instruct them to make for themselves
> fringes on the corners of their garments throughout the ages; let
> them attach a cord of blue to the fringe at each corner. That shall

be your fringe; look at it and recall all the commandments of the Lord and observe them, so that you do not follow your heart and eyes in your lustful urge. Thus you shall be reminded to observe all My commandments and to be holy to your God.

The tallit has a border of knotted fringe, the *tzitzit*. Each tzitzit is made of eight strands of thread. The rules for tying the tzitzit are ancient. One strand is wrapped around the others seven, eight, eleven, and thirteen times, with a knot separating each group. Many believe the numbers involved are significant, that associating each number with a letter of the Jewish alphabet spells the name of God, or that multiplying the numbers equals the number 613, the number of the Torah's laws one must obey.

Islamic prayer beads, meanwhile, are called either *masbaha* or *subha* ("to praise"). They originated in the seventh century after the prophet Muhammad proclaimed the ninety-nine names for God and promised "he who enumerates them would get into Paradise." Strands of either 33, 36, or 99 beads were probably adopted from Buddhism to facilitate counting the number of recitations of Allah's ninety-nine names.

Theoretically more than 1.5 billion Muslims stop their lives five times a day to face Mecca for the call to pray (*Allahu akbar. La Ilaha ila Allah wa Muhamadun rasul Allah . . .*), a practice similar to that of Christian Benedictine communities, who stop and pray five to eight times a day, and have been doing so since before the founding of Islam. What a powerful image of praise the wider world of Christians might contemplate emulating as they stroll Fifth Avenue or cross Atlanta's Peachtree Road. Imagine the Super Bowl and its beer commercials being interrupted by a call to prayer, with 115,000,000 Christians falling to their knees, nachos in hand, before flat-screen TVs to praise God, not football.

Other faith traditions that use prayer beads are Baha'i, Sikhism, and even modern forms of Paganism. Founded in the nineteenth century in Iran, Baha'i uses prayer beads of 95 beads of stone or wood, representing the 95 times a day to repeat *Allah u Abha*, a form of God's name. Many sets have a tassel or a nine-pointed star representing the faith's emblem. Founded in fifteenth-century India and based on the phrase *Ik Onkar* ("one God"), service, and rejection of the caste system, Sikhism is the world's ninth-largest religion, with more than 25,000,000 adherents. Identifiable by a turban that covers hair that is never cut, a Sikh is a "disciple" or "learner." Although many consider the number 108 to represent infinity, Sikh malas can contain any number of beads and are meant to serve as reminders of the divine through prayer or recitation of scripture. They are made of steel loops worn on either the shoulder or around the neck with steel or iron beads, on the wrist, looped over the shoulder, or even on the finger, depending on the number and size of beads used.

It is important to have a prefatory if rudimentary look at the rich background that existed before the Christian Desert Mothers and Fathers came to Egypt in the third century. The emphasis on numerology alone among all religions is fascinating and a subject in itself. Condensing three thousand years across the globe into only these few pages, however, smacks of a fifth-grade book report, and what is most missing from this too-brief overview of the non-Christian world religions' prayer beads is, of course, any sense of the thousands of years' cumulative passion prompting their use and of stories illustrating their continuing power in lives devoted to prayer.

2
If Lady Godiva Only Knew: Early Christian and Roman Catholic Prayer Beads

Once a month for quite a few years I have helped prepare the ingredients for Sunday's weekly Downtown Community Breakfast for the homeless at my church. I go in the quiet and anonymity of early Saturday morning, line up all my utensils and the trays of 360 eggs, and begin.

As I crack each of the eggs against the rim of one of the large vats—one-handed, and sometimes but rarely double-fisted—I think or say, *This one's for you, this one's for you*, in rhythm with the movement of my hands. I beat thirty eggs together at a time, folding in milk, and prefer a hand whisk to the electric mixer because it seems, inexplicably, more personal. It is a quiet ministry of prayer in the empty church, a rhythmic kinesis of body, mind, and heart.

This one's for you, this one's for you, I think, like counting beads on a string of prayer beads. But, because in other circumstances any one of the next morning's diners could be me—or you—and because I too have known inner homelessness, I sometimes say with the last egg, *This one's for me.*

Who would have thought the morning when I cracked my first egg I would eventually break and beat almost eighty thousand of them?

With prayer beads, it all began with pebbles.

Until Constantine signed an edict in 313 making Christianity legal, persecution of Christians was common. The threat of death and the increasing materialism seeping into Christian culture in the third century led many devout men and women to forgo life in civilization and seek the Egyptian, Palestinian, and Syrian deserts to live as hermits. They devoted their lives to a demanding asceticism and prayer in a wilderness rife with scorpions and poisonous vipers, a wilderness marked by darkness, loneliness, hunger, heat and cold—and an absence of hygiene.

The world—other than Benedictine monastic orders—knew little about the lives of these Desert Fathers and Mothers until Trappist monk Thomas Merton's affectionate 1960 book, *The Wisdom of the Desert: Sayings from the Desert Fathers of the Fourth Century*. The 1984 publication of the first comprehensive translation of their sayings—Benedicta Ward's *The Sayings of the Desert Fathers*—along with Henri Nouwen's *The Way of the Heart* and, more recently, the online Abbey of the Art's Christine Valters Paintner's *Desert Fathers and Mothers* have directed new attention to the spirituality of these ancients. Franciscan author and theologian Richard Rohr's daily emails are spurring increased interest in the silence, simplicity, and deep commitment of these wilderness dwellers and the richness of sparcity that marked their lives. It is important that you be introduced to three of these influential eremites of prayer.

Although the three monks mentioned here are men, many women—though fewer in number—were also influential during this period. They are not as highlighted in the histories because, of course, society was patriarchal, historians were male, and histories were written for a male monastic audience. Amma (Mother) Syncletica of

Alexandria, Theodora of Alexandria, and Amma Sarah of the Desert, for instance, led notable lives, as did Melania the Elder and the Younger, Olympias, and St. Paula and her daughter Eustochium. Although not household names, they contributed forty-seven quotations to *The Sayings of the Desert Fathers* but are not discussed here because they are not related to a history of prayer beads per se—nor is the fascinating St. Thecla, a first-century disciple and companion of the apostle Paul. (Condemned to being tossed to the lions by her own mother for her refusal to marry, the young virgin was saved, according to legend, by female lions ganging up against the male ones in the Colosseum. She reportedly lived in a cave in the Turkish wilderness near Ephesus as a hermit for seventy-two years after her second miraculous rescue from death. Her life is recounted in the apocryphal *Acts of Paul and Thecla*, and a recently exposed, lifelike and life-sized mosaic of Thecla and Paul can be seen in a cave above Ephesus. She is known as the first female evangelist, but she and other Desert Mothers are for another story.)

Tradition states that Paul of Thebes, generally identified as the first desert hermit, lived in an Egyptian wilderness cave until his death in the year 342 at age 113. Clothed in palm leaves and eating only dates and bread brought to him by a raven, he was committed to praying 300 Psalms—the 150 Psalms twice—a day. In order to keep count of the number of prayer he was on, he and many other Desert Fathers carried 300 pebbles in their cloaks and, after each prayer, tossed out one of the pebbles. This cumbersome and inefficient method marks the beginning of Christian prayer-counting that eventually led to the creation of the Eastern Orthodox prayer rope and the Catholic rosary—and eventually, of course, to Protestant prayer beads.

The Egyptian Coptic St. Anthony the Great is usually credited with establishing the monastic movement. Although he himself did not found a monastery, by the time of his death, *hundreds of thousands* of devout seekers had made their way to the western Egyptian Nitrian desert to live in cenobitic communities or as hermits. The original desert-seekers were less than pleased with this influx into their solitude.

St. Anthony is particularly known for his design of the knots themselves of the prayer rope used by Eastern Orthodox Christians today. Legend has it that he was beset by demons of wild animals and phantoms of women, as well as the demons of laziness and boredom. Frustrated by not knowing how to keep up with his prayers when distracted, he heard a voice calling him outside, where he saw an angel weaving palm leaves and then sitting to pray, and weaving palm leaves again and then sitting to pray again. "Do this," he was told, "and you will be saved."

But Anthony continued to be troubled by Satan, who, according to the legend, would untie each of the knots of prayer on the leather strap Anthony kept until Anthony finally tied a knotted cross within each knot. Satan could not bear the sign of the cross and fled. Almost twenty-four hundred years later, his design for tying the knots is still used today. YouTube has excellent videos demonstrating how to tie these complicated marks of prayer.

St. Pachomius the Great, a former Roman soldier, established the first known organized monastery with rules. He and Anthony established a monastic pattern used centuries later by Benedict in the West and Mt. Athos in the East, and Pachomius is credited with incorporating the use of the prayer rope used today. *Komboskini* in Greek, *tchotki* in Russian—of 10, 12, 33, 50, 150, 300, and 500 knots, depending on one's prayer rule—prayer ropes are usually of black wool. Some have beads interwoven to aid in keeping track of counting. It is, however,

considered ostentatious to wear them—a custom contradictory to the lavish displays of expensively jeweled prayer beads of Henry VIII's time that we will look at later.

Because most people were illiterate and memorizing 150 Psalms a challenge, prayer most often was a repetition of what is known as The Prayer of the Heart, or Jesus Prayer ("Lord Jesus Christ, Son of God, have mercy on me, a sinner"), still recited today and attributed to the Desert Fathers. For those like the Desert Fathers, who did not attend services or use service books or were illiterate, one could replace the parts of a service with the Jesus Prayer. One's knees weaken at the challenge:

- Instead of the entire Psalter: 6,000 Jesus Prayers
- One kathisma of the Psalter: 300 prayers (100 for each stasis)
- Midnight office: 600
- Matins: 1500
- The hours without the inter-hours: 1,000
- The hours with the inter-hours: 1,500
- Vespers: 600
- Great Compline: 700
- Small Compline: 400
- A canon or akathist to the Most Holy Theotokos (Mother of God): 500

Most of us living with the tinsel, pace, and seductions of the Western world reel at the thought of this practice and the commitment of one's life to this level of austerity, silence, and solitude. It gives one pause to think of the escapist activities and thoughts we substitute. And what, one wonders, would St. Paul of Thebes make of an iPhone—or even clothes?

The word *Rosary* refers to the prayers said while using the *rosary*, a string of prayer beads themselves. Some Roman Catholics credit the origin of the rosary to the Castilian monk St. Dominic, founder of the Order of Preachers known as the Dominican Order, who had a vision in which the Virgin Mary, who smelled like roses, handed him the beads in the year 1214. Older accounts of rosaries already in use exist, however: A Belgium museum claims a set of strung prayer beads that belonged to the seventh-century abbess Gertrude of Nivelles, patron saint of cats and the mentally ill (a pairing some may find apt or humorous).

In the sixth century Benedict prescribed the recitation of the 150 Psalms once a week for monks and nuns; memorizing them all proved too difficult for many, so a psalter of 150 repetitions of the Our Father (the *Pater Noster*) and, later, a psalter of 150 repetitions of the Hail Mary developed. A string of beads was used to keep count. In 1250 Thomas of Contimpre coined the term *rosary* for these prayers and beads. Although there are many other forms of rosaries or "chaplets" with differing arrangements and numbers of beads—from the seven-decade Franciscan rosary to the one-decade rosary ring—the most prevalent form contains five sets of ten beads, called *decades*, with each decade preceded by a larger bead called a *gaud* (source of both our words *gaudy* and *joy*) and ending in five beads leading to the crucifix.

The earliest written record of a rosary is the one Godgifu, Lady Godiva, Countess of Mercia, willed at her death around 1040 to a monastery in Coventry—one of the many she and her husband, Leofric, founded. Described as a "circlet of gems which she had threaded on a string in order that by fingering them one-by-one as she successively recited her prayers, she might not fall short of the exact number," the necklace was hung around the neck of the monastery's statue of Mary. The convent, statue, and necklace no longer exist, so the written description is historically noteworthy.

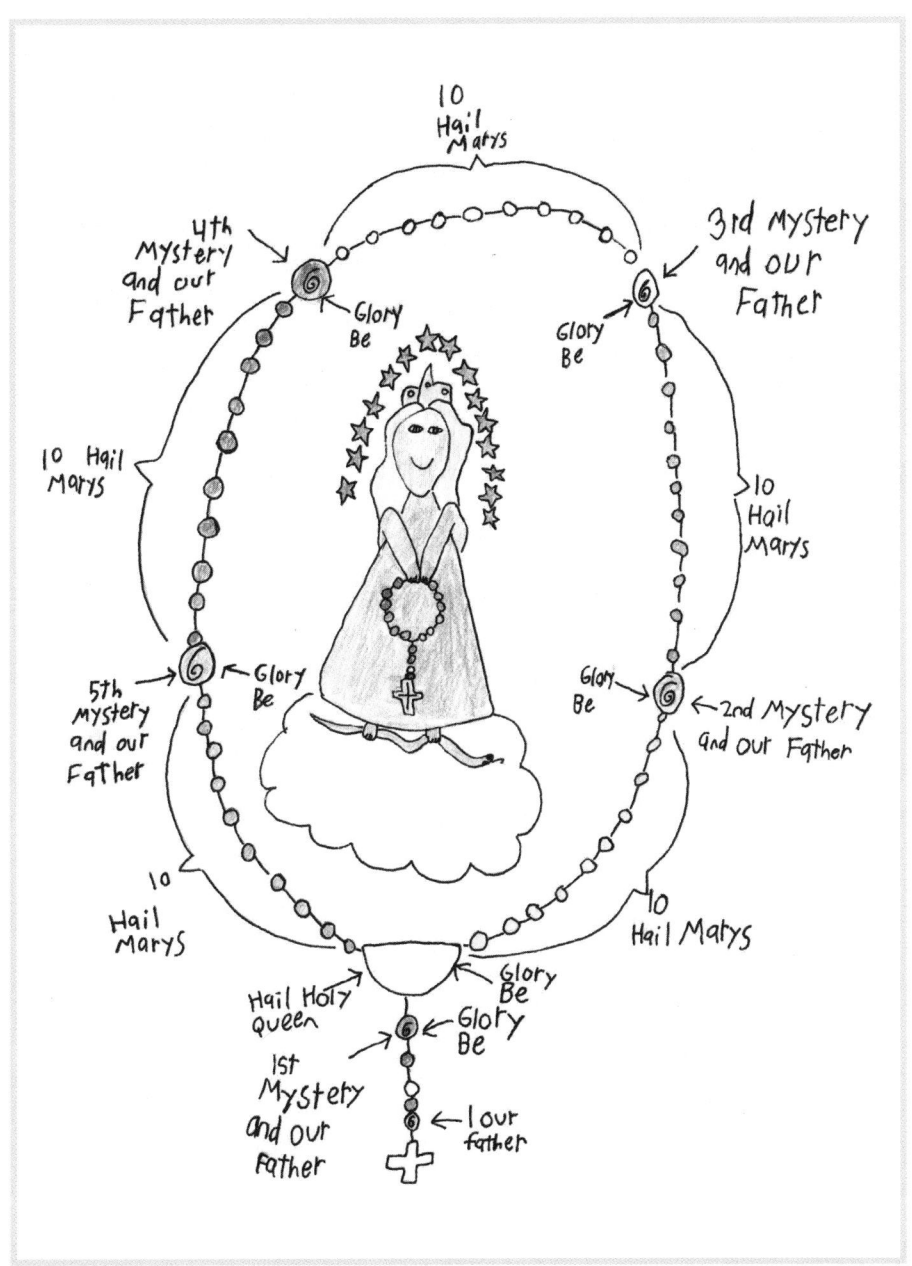

10
Hail
Marys

4th
Mystery
and our
Father

Glory
Be

3rd Mystery
and our
Father

Glory
Be

10 Hail
Marys

10
Hail
Marys

Glory
Be

5th
Mystery
and our
Father

Glory
Be

2nd Mystery
and our Father

10
Hail
Marys

10 Hail Marys

Hail Holy
Queen

Glory
Be

Glory
Be

1st
Mystery
and our
Father

1 our
father

Although the popular legend about her ride through Coventry is considered by most historians to be just that, a legend, her beneficence is seen in the supposed reason for her ride. Begging her husband not to tax the overburdened citizens of Coventry, Godiva, who was possibly the wealthiest woman in England, agreed to ride through the streets naked in response to her husband's taunt. Due to the reverence the townspeople felt for her honor and compassion, all closed their shutters, except for one Peeping Tom—source of the famous phrase we still use today.

Lady Godiva's rosary was made of prized jewels. Until the Reformation, religious jewelry was not taxed, so many rosaries were composed of precious gems worn draped over the shoulder or hanging from the waist as conspicuous testaments of wealth—as well as tokens of tax evasion.

Today an estimated 1.2 billion Roman Catholics of the world pray on rosaries, whether made of plastic, simple olive wood, or more prized gemstones. Because we are told that we must come as children, on the previous page is a child's drawing of the parts of the most common form of the Catholic rosary. The figure in the center is Mother Mary, who is so happy to see you.

3
Protestant Prayer Beads

We need to remember that the Catholic rosary is part of the history of Protestants as well as of Catholics. Until the Reformation, when Catholicism and its outward manifestations were outlawed, all Protestants were of course Catholic, and rosaries were central to their lives. Peri-reformers and reformers inveighed against the "popish" rosary, however, particularly due to its association with the concept and practice of indulgences. Because prosecution for being caught with one could be severe, single-string beads of one decade—or chaplets, shorter than the rosary—hanging from a ring and ending in a crucifix could easily be hidden up a sleeve.

Although there have always been Protestants and those of other religions who have used the Catholic rosary—particularly due to its association with the nurturing nature of the Virgin Mary—it is not a common practice, and many Protestants have retained a Reformation attitude about it.

Hundreds of years passed before Lynn Bauman and a retreat group associated with Good Shepherd Episcopal Church in Cedar Hill, Texas, met in 1987 to design a set of Anglican prayer beads. One of Bauman's aims was to draw Eastern and Western churches closer; the cross he used is a San Damiano cross, often associated

with St. Francis of Assisi, a saint who has always drawn Christians together. Since then, interest in the beads among all denominations has increased exponentially, and Episcopal prayer beads are now often called simply Protestant prayer beads. Bauman continues to produce the original Anglican rosary at his Praxis retreat community in Telephone, Texas. I enjoy the irony of thinking that prayer beads are indeed a metaphorical telephone.

Martin Luther was a Catholic Augustinian friar who did not want to leave the Catholic Church but was excommunicated. Even so, he continued to pray with his rosary, although shortening the Hail Mary's. The current Evangelical Lutheran Church of America encourages members to pray with prayer beads. The Pearls of Life or Wreath of Christ rosary of eighteen beads was developed in 1995 by Swedish bishop emeritus Martin Lönnebo, and a Lutheran rosary similar to the Roman Catholic one was designed by seminarian John Longworth in 2005 to be prayed with Luther's *Small Catechism*.

Other forms of rosaries, each with a different purpose, are numerous. Some of the less well-known types in use are the Angelic Trisagion Chaplet, Brigittine Rosary, Chaplet of Divine Mercy, Coptic Mequtaria, Croatian Peace Chaplet, Dominican Rosary, Franciscan Crown Rosary, Gifts of the Holy Spirit Chaplet, Irish Penal Rosary, Lazo Wedding Rosary, Psalms of Hope Chaplet, Psalter and Paternoster, Seven Dolor Rosary, and Stella Maris Chaplet. And the list goes on, a testament to different universal needs.

Drawing elements from the design and purpose of all other major religions' prayer beads, Anglican/Episcopal or Protestant beads are circular, beginning with a sacred object, usually a cross, followed by an Invitatory bead, which invites the user to pray and invokes God's presence.

The user then enters the circle of 32 beads arranged in four groups of seven with four larger beads separating each of the smaller seven beads' groups, for a total of 33 beads, the number of years of Christ's life on earth. Smaller spacer beads can be used before and after each larger bead as demarcation, as well as between the cross, the Invitatory bead, and the beginning of the circle.

Bauman named the four groups of seven beads "the Weeks." They represent the seven days of the week; the number of perfection; the number of church sacraments—baptism, confirmation, communion, ordination, marriage, confession, and anointing of the sick; and the seven seasons of the church calendar—Advent, Christmas, Epiphany, Lent, Holy Week, Easter, and Pentecost. Bauman's intention was that the beads be used every day, every week, all year. He also proscribed that no set words or prayers be associated with the set of beads.

When the beads are spread out in a circle, the four larger beads form a cross, which is why these beads are called Cruciform beads. They represent the four times of daily prayer in the Episcopal Book of Common Prayer—morning, noonday, evening, and compline; the number of the seasons; the four elements—earth, wind, fire, and water; the four directions; the four cardinal virtues—prudence, justice, fortitude, and temperance; and the four Gospels—Matthew, Mark, Luke, and John.

Again, as a reminder that we are to come as children (Matthew 18:3), this drawing of a set of Anglican/Protestant prayer beads is by a child. The figure in the middle is a welcoming Jesus.

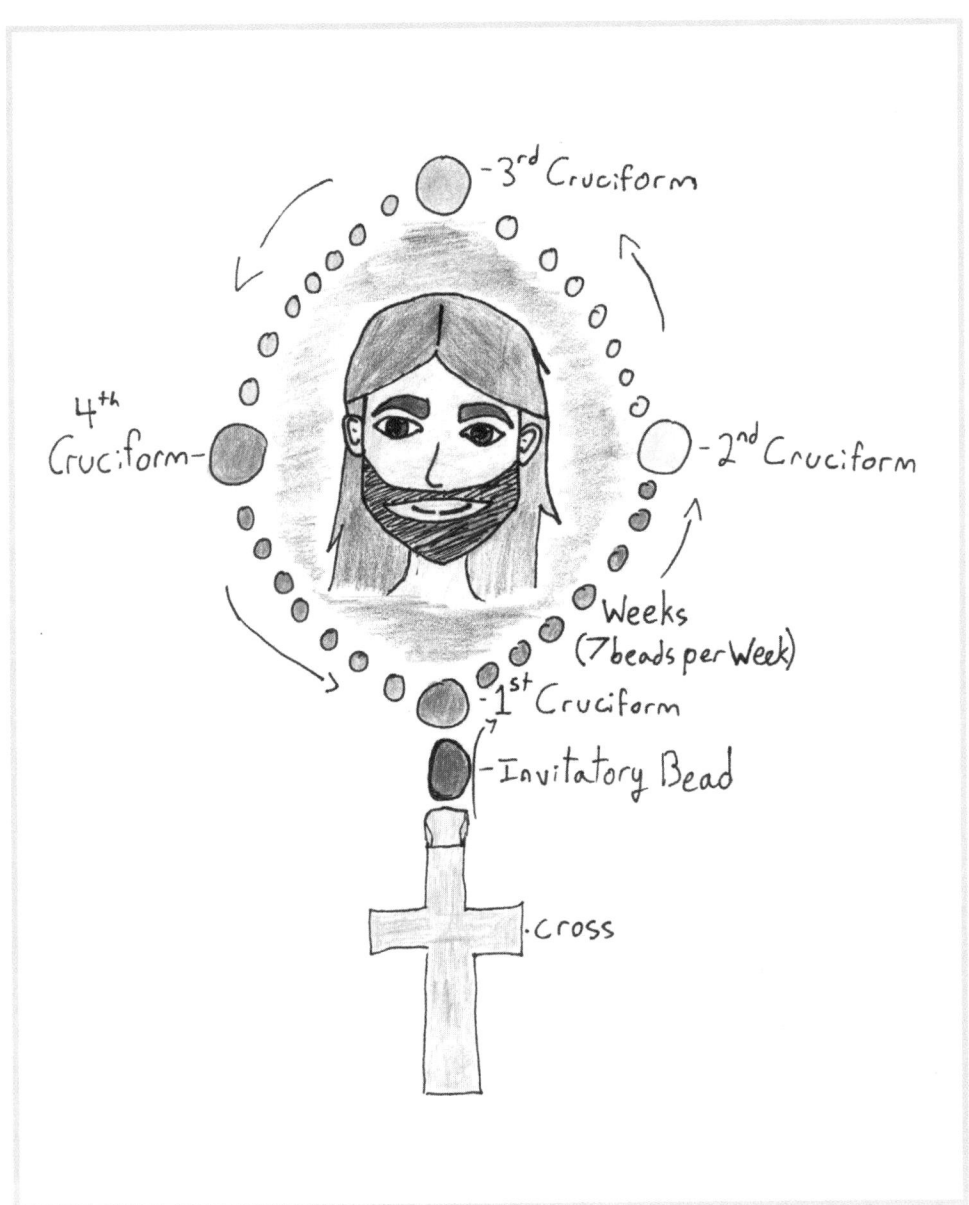

Although there is no set way to pray with the beads—many people simply hold them, lightly or tightly, in their hands or run their fingers across the different textures of the various beads while trying to clear their minds and hearts—others prefer the security of knowing a pattern to follow and the exact prayers to pray. Rote repetition is a double-edged sword, though. It can free the mind—which is the objective of contemplative prayer as explained by Trappist monks Thomas Merton and Thomas Keating and, more recently, Richard Rohr—to simply shut up and listen for your God to show up. The flip side of memorized prayer, however, is how easy it is to fool oneself into *thinking* one is actually praying and to check off that little box of the day's to-do list, when all one has done is make a gesture of empty words.

Although I love much about the rich language of my Episcopal liturgy, even with its ceaseless demand for the wealth of metaphors I must conjure up—the confession, snippets of the Eucharist prayers, the post-communion prayer, the benediction—bottom line, I find I am still a closet Southern Baptist when it comes to prayer. The Baptist tradition of my youth contained no hellfire, brimstone, condemnation, or exclusion. I simply learned to pray spontaneously and fervently—on a dime. Moreover, many of us in the South are also deeply appreciative of being surrounded by the insights and rhythms of prayer, often punctuated by snare drums, of many African American churches in our communities. God must take particular delight in certain Southern Sunday morning worship services.

When I was a child, church prayers seemed endless, and many of them were stentorian compositions. When finally graduating to the big table for Thanksgiving and Christmas at my grandparents' house, I thought my grandfather Honey Pop was going to pray for every cotton plant and mule in Cross County, Arkansas. I'd check through half-closed eyes to see if everyone else's eyes were closed, heads bowed, Norman Rockwell expressions properly serious, and then I'd slip my hand out of my brother's, smush at embroidered buds and leaves on my great-grandmother's tablecloth with my knife, and pick at the threads of entredeux with the knife's tip while Honey Pop drawled a year's worth of deep thanks about family, friends, crops, and weather.

That tablecloth has served through six generations of prayer and rites of passage. I am now its keeper for the next generation. For a while I used it as the coverlet on my bed, a shroud and a swaddling cloth of memories, and went to sleep each night blanketed in prayer. And then I got a cat, so the tablecloth—with its faint stains of wine and cranberry, hieroglyphs charting the passing years of love at that table—is packed away with its stories until it's time for a holiday celebration.

Looking back at all those years, edged now, of course, in memory's idealized soft glow, I realize that when my grandfather prayed, he seemed simply to be talking to a close family friend. I did not realize it then, but it was as though the Holy Spirit had dressed up, too, for Thanksgiving with my family and must have cared deeply about Arkansas rain and mules, looking forward to the after-dinner cigar he'd smoke with my grandfather.

I don't often pray today about cotton, soy beans, and tractors, but I do find myself chatting—sometimes even gossiping—with the Universe when I pray. And these days I find, more often than not, it's a thanks-giving.

Bauman's original aim was that there be no prescribed prayers to say when praying with the beads and that each person develop individual prayers and even the way to move the beads in the hand. Many people simply freeze and flounder, however, when given the option to create their own system. The next two chapters highlight a few prayers for you to consider using.

4
Clearing Your Cache and Beginning to Pray

Regardless of how many years and how earnestly you have prayed, author John McQuiston reminds us, "Always We Begin Again." Each attempt at prayer is a new one. There are no referees, no winning score, no out-of-bounds, no penalties. You must bring your whole self to it. Several years ago I heard Richard Rohr say, "I have prayed for years for one good humiliation a day, and then, I must watch my reaction to it. I have no other way of spotting both my denied shadow self and my idealized persona." Prayer can be messy. It is not—and should not be, I believe—a tidy package. We must wade through the mud first. As Buddhist teacher Thich Nhat Hanh reminds us, "no mud, no lotus."

Jesus tells us in Matthew 6:5–6 to go into our closet to pray. Closets are of course our first choice as children when playing Hide and Seek, and that often describes prayer: Hide and Seek. And we are still children. However, I retreat at the image of the Holy Spirit in my closet—ancient dust balls roiling among the cluttered clogs and worn-out sandals, pants legs slapping about, a sweater or two slumped off hangers—and the two of us hunkering knee to knee amid the musty odor of tee shirts and jeans whining, "Put me in the laundry!" This closet with its housekeeping embarrassments of course is the untidy closet of my heart. And, as messy as it might be, this is exactly where we all must begin. One of the main points of prayer, it seems to me, is in fact to air our dirty laundry.

We can spend a lot of time and effort hiding from what we know to face in prayer—"That of which we are not aware, owns us," James Hollis reminds us in *Finding Meaning in the Second Half of Life*—but sometimes roles switch; the Spirit sometimes seems to hide, sometimes for months, even for years.

In 1989 Mother Teresa came to Memphis to speak. Two of my children were quite young and could have no idea at the time of the enormity of devotion and accomplishment of this tiny woman, but I wanted them to have a memory of her presence. For some lucky reason we were given aisle seats. We waited a long, very fidgety time. Suddenly there was a stir. Mother Teresa did not come out on a stage two hundred feet away but was actually walking up the aisle toward us. The packed coliseum was quiet with respect and awe as she approached. Then she was beside us, and my son Walker, in the carrying voice of an excited child, stood up and exclaimed to the hushed auditorium, "Look, Mom, she has on sandals! And they're just like mine!"

We now know that Mother Teresa, as many of us do, experienced her own very dark night of the soul. According to her letters—which she never believed would be made public—the desolation and abandonment by God she felt lasted for fifty years, beginning almost from the moment she arrived in Calcutta to begin the work she believed Jesus had commanded her to do. Continuing her work, and always smiling ("a mask," she called it), she wrote of the "torture," "emptiness," and "darkness" she lived with for the majority of her life. For a period she even stopped praying. We balk and flounder, searching for an adequate explanation for this gut-wrenching information—or dismiss it with a shrug of psychological shoulders. As unutterably painful as those years must have been for her, though, they tell each of us in our own dark nights of searing doubt and unbearable loneliness that we're in good company. We all wear the same sandals.

When deciding on a space to use to pray with your beads, choose a place where you feel both physically and emotionally comfortable and will not be interrupted during the time you've set aside for praying. This can be a difficult order for those with children at home (ironically, a time in life when you probably need even more time to pray).

Sit quietly and simply hold the beads in your hand. Clear the cache of your mind's computer. When you start thinking about your grocery list or what you will wear later, redirect your mind to your hands. Hold the cross, or other object sacred to you, by both hands and think of what name you want to call your God, your Lover. Do not be squeamish. Try out several names, either silently or out loud. You might be surprised at what pops out of your mouth. No one will hear you. You do not have to use the same name every day, and the tone of voice in your head might change from day to day depending on your mood and the feeling you have for this relationship. Some days you might feel beseeching; others, hesitant, chummy, or angry. Just bring yourself to this meeting. Even David, more than three thousand years ago in Psalm 139:1–3, knew:

> O LORD, you have searched me and known me.
> You know when I sit down and when I rise up;
> you discern my thoughts from far away.

You search out my path and my lying down,

and are acquainted with all my ways.

After holding the cross, next move your hand to the Invitatory bead. Run your right thumb over it, inviting your God into your physical as well as emotional space. Several years ago the Reverend Gay Rahn was a priest at my church. She often kept us on our toes and in one particular sermon presented an idea that has stayed with me over the years about inviting the Holy into your day. She told us to imagine that Jesus was coming to our house and we were to decorate a room for him. That, she said, would give us each an idea of who our Jesus is. As a designer, I immediately whipped into gear. Chintz was the first discard. Who, I thought, would possibly choose chintz for Jesus! Over the years I've run through unbleached linen slipcovers, thrown out any definable period furniture, switched back and forth between sisal carpeting and wide-plank hardwood—and then decided on using both—and then even played with giving chintz a chance (who, living with all that monotone, flowerless desert landscape, I realized, wouldn't feel refreshed, surrounded by bright, down-cushioned old English chintz?). I've even debated styles of glassware, whether to serve wine or beer, sweet or unsweet tea, whether to use sterling or stainless, what variety of flowers I'd choose for a vase, and even what books to stack on the floor. It's been intriguing to see my choices change over the years and to weigh the reasons for those choices. The point here, of course, is that you're inviting your God into your heart, your figurative home. And that's what you do now. Ask God to come sit on your couch with the fraying seams or plop down beside you on the floor by your bed, and y'all chat awhile.

After you have invited God into your day holding the Invitatory bead, reach next for the first Cruciform bead. Choose a prayer or word or line of Scripture or poetry to think or say while holding it. You can repeat it for each of the four Cruciform beads, or choose a new line or even a whole poem for each different Cruciform bead.

Then, moving counter-clockwise, run each of the seven Weeks beads between your thumb and forefinger. Be aware of the different textures and the coolness or warmth. Be aware you are one in a thousands-year line of myriads of different peoples who have spent part of their days doing just what you're doing. The metaphorical dishes in their sinks waited too. Talking to their God and cleaning their mind was more important than cleaning house.

Many people traditionally repeat the same short prayer—often what is known as the Jesus Prayer ("Lord Jesus Christ, Son of God, have mercy on me, a sinner") that originated with the Desert Fathers—while others choose a longer verse like the Lord's Prayer or the Apostles' Creed to say while their fingers move over all seven beads.

Repeat your chosen prayers as you come to each of the beads until you come to the end. Some people go around the circle three times, as acknowledgment of the Trinity and to emulate the one hundred prayers of the Eastern Orthodox Church; others go around only once. When you are ready to exit the beads, skip the first Cruciform bead and move down again to the Invitatory bead, say its prayer, and move to the cross. You can say the same prayer with the cross that you began with, or you can end your prayers with a "goodbye" prayer. Some people end their session by kissing the cross. Others simply give it a squeeze or draw it to their heart.

Remember that when Bauman designed the Anglican or Protestant prayer bead set, he did not want specific prayers identified with the beads. He wanted each user to devise his or her own prayers. However, because many people feel uncomfortable when confronted with infinite choices, we'll next look at suggestions of more prayers you might want to try.

5
Prayers, Poems, Lectio, Music, Silence

What is prayer? You take words, everyday words, and all of a sudden they become holy. Why? Because there is something that separates one word from another and then you try to fill the vacuum. With what? With whom? With what memory? With what aspiration? So when words bring you closer to the prisoner in his cell, to the patient who is dying on his bed alone, to the starving child, then it's a prayer.

—Elie Wiesel

Whether you use actual words, a mantra, or silence—or vary your method from day to day—is your choice. You can approach your prayers either with the intention of concentrating on the words' meanings or as a contemplative, centering practice to free your mind—and to listen.

Because prayer is such a highly personal experience, you are also encouraged to write your own forms. If you hem and haw and think, *Oh shucks, I can't do that,* of course you can. God was not an English major. Making connection is the point. Personally, I wish I could channel the late Representative Barbara Jordan to do all my praying for me, or borrow her marvelously resonant voice instead of my own puny one. (If I were God, I'd sit up really straight and pay close attention if Ms. Jordan were talking to me.)

Richard Rohr believes we in the West have turned prayer into a left-brain activity. "Prayer is a state of union," he says, "of communion either in words or more probably in silence. When we are not in union, regardless of what words we may be saying, it is not prayer." He also cautions us that "a lot of us pray as if prayer is really twisting the arm of God or convincing God to do something. We think by saying more words we'll talk God into it. We think, 'If I say it one more time, God will agree with me.'" Rohr notes "there is something compassionate about asking God to heal your grandmother; of course that's beautiful. But it is still you in the driver's seat and trying to get God in your driver's seat."

Because we become different selves as we mature spiritually, don't get locked into only considering the same prayers you've always said. Be on the lookout for new ways to express who you are becoming. Keep a journal, perhaps, of new ideas and lines of thoughts you can incorporate. I have kept a folder of quotes, Scripture, and poems on my computer desktop since 1997. An unintended consequence of this collection is its charting of my spiritual self over these years. Sometimes I'll read one of the poems and think, *Oh, my heavens, why in the world did I ever want to copy this one? It's really silly.* Other times I'll come across one I haven't read in a while and feel as though the top of my head will pop off, thinking, *Wow. Yes. Wow. Oh wow. Hello again!*

What follows is a very brief selection of mainly well known prayers to consider pairing with your beads.

Traditional Prayers to Go with Beads

Agnus Dei ("Lamb of God") Prayer

THE CROSS

> The Lord's Prayer

THE INVITATORY

> "Let the words of my mouth and the meditation of my heart be acceptable in your sight, O LORD, my strength and my redeemer." (Psalm 19:14)

THE CRUCIFORMS

> O Lamb of God that takest away the sins of the world, have mercy upon us. O Lamb of God that takest away the sins of the world, have mercy upon us. O Lamb of God that takest away the sins of the world, grant us peace.

THE WEEKS

> Almighty and merciful Lord, Father, Son, and Holy Spirit, bless us and keep us. Amen.

A Celtic Prayer

THE CROSS

> In the Name of God, Father, Son, and Holy Spirit. Amen.

THE INVITATORY

> O God make speed to save me (us),
>
> O Lord make haste to help me (us),

Glory to the Father, and to the Son, and to the Holy Spirit:

As it was in the beginning, is now, and will be forever. Amen.

THE CRUCIFORMS

Be the eye of God dwelling with me, the foot of Christ in guidance with me, the shower of the Spirit pouring on me, richly and generously.

THE WEEKS

I bow before the Father who made me,

I bow before the Son who saved me,

I bow before the Spirit who guides me,

In love and adoration.

I praise the Name of the one on high.

I bow before thee, Sacred Three,

The ever One, the Trinity.

THE INVITATORY

The Lord's Prayer

THE CROSS

Bless the Lord. Thanks be to God.

Julian of Norwich Prayer

THE CROSS

In the Name of God, Father, Son, and Holy Spirit. Amen.

THE INVITATORY

O God make speed to save me (us),

O Lord make haste to help me (us),

Glory to the Father, and to the Son, and to the Holy Spirit:

As it was in the beginning, is now, and will be forever. Amen.

God of your goodness, give me yourself,

For you are enough to me.

And I can ask for nothing less that is to your glory.

And if I ask for anything less, I shall still be in want, for only in you have

I all.

THE WEEKS

All shall be well, and all shall be well, and all manner of things shall be well.

THE INVITATORY

The Lord's Prayer

THE CROSS

Bless the Lord. Thanks be to God.

Other Prayers for Common Occasions

Prayer of Confession

Most merciful God, we confess that we have sinned against you in thought, word, and deed, by what we have done, and by what we have left undone. We have not loved you with our whole heart; we have not loved our neighbors as ourselves. We are truly sorry and we humbly repent. For the sake of your Son Jesus Christ, have mercy on us and forgive us; that we may delight in your will, and walk in your ways, to the glory of your Name. (The Book of Common Prayer)

For Protection

The Lord is my shepherd; I shall not want.

He maketh me to lie down in green pastures: he leadeth me beside the still waters.

He restoreth my soul: he leadeth me in the paths of righteousness for his name's sake.

Yea, though I walk through the valley of the shadow of death, I will fear no evil: for thou art with me; thy rod and thy staff they comfort me.

Thou preparest a table before me in the presence of mine enemies: thou anointest my head with oil; my cup runneth over.

Surely goodness and mercy shall follow me all the days of my life: and I will dwell in the house of the Lord for ever. (Psalm 23, KJV)

For Peace

Anne Lamott calls this prayer, attributed to Reinhold Niebuhr, "a Greatest Hits prayer" and a "reset button prayer."

THE SERENITY PRAYER

God grant me the serenity to accept the things I cannot change, courage to change the things I can, and wisdom to know the difference.

For Guidance

My Lord God, I have no idea where I am going. I do not see the road ahead of me. I cannot know for certain where it will end. Nor do I really know myself, and the fact that I think that I am following your will does not mean that I am actually doing so. But I believe that the desire to please you does in fact please you. And I hope I have that desire in all that I am doing. I hope that I will never do anything apart from that desire. And I know that if I do this, you will lead me by the right road, though I may

know nothing about it. Therefore will I trust you always, though I may seem to be lost and in the shadow of death. I will not fear, for you are ever with me, and you will never leave me to face my perils alone. (Thomas Merton, from *Thoughts in Solitude*)

For Passion

PRAYER OF ST. ANSELM

Let me see you in my desire,

Let me desire you in my seeking.

Let me find you by loving you,

Let me love you when I find you.

Lectio Divina Exercise with Your Beads

Take a few deep breaths. Prepare to say, "Be still and know that I am God" (Psalm 46:10) in five diminishing lines:

   * Say or think, "Be still and know that I am God."
   * Take a couple of slow, deep breaths and say, "Be still and know that I am."
   * Take a couple of slow, deep breaths and say, "Be still and know."
   * Take a couple of slow, deep breaths and say, "Be still."
   * Take a couple of slow, deep breaths and say, "Be."
   * Sit still and breathe, and when ready, say, "Amen."

Music and Silence: When There Are No Words

Hymns

Make a list of your favorite hymns. A plethora of hymns exists that speak to any of the four types of prayer. You can say just the words, hum the melody, or burst into song, regardless of your talent. (The words of many hymns, of course, are just awful, either because the insipid author lacks talent or because the words and actions are bloody and violent, so you might want to just hum.) Although in church people tend to move farther away down the pew from me when we hit the first bar of any hymn, I sing—and dance—when home alone. You can too.

Chant

Turn to chant, from the Taize Community, an ecumenical monastic order of Catholics and Protestants in Burgundy, France. Key in "Taize" on YouTube and listen to several of the more popular selections (i.e., the ones with the highest number of listeners noted under the title). Simply listen, perhaps with your eyes closed, as you pass the beads between your fingers, or memorize one that appeals to you to sing on your own. The music of the chants is inseparable from the words.

Classical Music and Opera

British playwright and poet William Congreve predated Bach, Beethoven, and Mozart when he said, "Musick has charms to soothe a savage breast." I know nothing about God's breast, but we all, including God I think, need periodic soothing in our frenzied, unpredictable lives. That the Universe wired our brains to create music leaves me speechless, which is what good music itself does—leaves us speechless, lights a fire in the core of our souls, and lays us bare. It speaks to us where words cannot go. Bach's deceptively simple fugues, Barber's wrenching *Adagio for Strings*,

Leontyne Price's Doretta's aria from Puccini's *La Rondine*, Pavarotti's "Nessun Dorma"—the list can go on and on. (Opera plots themselves—or even the lyrics—do not count, though; W. H. Auden reminds us that "No opera plot can be sensible, for people do not sing when they are feeling sensible.") Only the music.

Choose any piece—orchestral, chamber, opera. Again, YouTube is invaluable—and use the beads in your hands to accompany, as though you are the conductor or first violin. Feel the vibration of Domingo's voice or Casal's or Yo-Yo Ma's cello in the beads themselves as well as in your heart. You and Bach or Pavarotti are putting on a private performance for the God who created this amazing gift that should never be taken for granted, that can bring us to our knees, that can anoint the top of our heads.

6
Praying the Beads
Without the Beads

*There are hundreds of ways to
kneel and kiss the ground.*

—Rumi

Unless one is a monk, prayer beads are rarely ever-present, particularly not during the frazzle and noise of most of our daily lives. If you're like me, you lose them in the bottom of your purse among breath-mint wrappers or remember you left them on the kitchen table. But you don't have to have them with you. Daily life and the mundane offer surprising opportunities to pray without ceasing with both body and heart, and often in unexpected ways.

Several years ago at a small dinner with author Sophy Burnham, I self-righteously snooted my disregard for people who prayed for parking places when there were so many other people and situations that needed help. Sophy reared up in her chair, leaned toward me with knife and fork poised in mid-air, and snorted, "What

pretension! How do you possibly think you control what prayers God should listen to! Pray for anything, everything!"

So now, of course, I do.

I invite you to consider some of the following opportunities—a couple of which might challenge your usual prayer routines in order to get your attention—and to devise ones of your own. Stretch!

The Blessing of the Lemons

For some, grocery shopping is creative therapy; for others of us, a dreaded, tedious trek. We've been there, done that, more than once too often: Into the basket, out of the basket onto the checkout stand, into the bags, into the car, into the house, and into the fridge and cabinets. And then you have to get it all out again—and cook. And then clean up. However, I learned on a recent visit that grocery shopping also offers itself as a weekly prayer-bead adventure.

The produce section particularly is alive with opportunities. Lemons appeal to me, but limes, oranges, red peppers, potatoes, onions, brussel sprouts, and eggplants also exhibit a come-hither look. Whether you enter the store with a hopeless sigh or with the bounce of anticipation, plant your feet in front of that large, mounded hill of lemon sunshine. Grasp a lemon, say a prayer; hold or touch another, say a prayer. Move in a circuit as though you're praying your beads. You can do this with eyes closed or open. Any other shoppers who pass and notice you will merely think you're an exacting shopper. If you think saying a whole set of lemon beads is too prolonged, simply wrap your fingers around only one, say a short prayer, and then move on to oranges.

Passing the pile of eggplant, wave to the Holy Spirit.

I particularly like praying with fruits because of the allusion to "fruits of the spirit." You can use the whole aisle of canned vegetables or soups, too, lightly running your fingers along the row of rounded bean cans as you maneuver your cart down the aisle. You can repeat a single word or thought, or move from prayer to prayer.

On several occasions writer Richard Rohr has recounted an experience while shopping where he found

> an ordinary moment is totally satisfying and more than enough. One day I experienced this in a local Kmart! I "came to" and found myself happily standing in an aisle just looking at boxes of Tide. I don't know how long I stood there. But there I was just smiling at the Tide boxes! Life was all utterly okay. I was okay and all was right with the world (and this was after a day of emotional trials). Just buying detergent had the effect that church was supposed to have! Some fellow shoppers probably thought I was on drugs!

Rohr found his moment with Tide laundry detergent. Lemons or canned peas can suffice too.

You can also turn the whole store into a prayer store, wordlessly blessing or acknowledging the Cosmic Christ within each person coming toward you down the aisle, remembering Gandhi's maxim that if you don't see God in the face of the next person you see, there's no point in looking any further.

This grocery exercise might be difficult the first time you try it, but think of the gift of the bounty of our earth you're surrounded by, and drop your self-consciousness. Yes, find Christ shopping among the canned peas. And, if you're not put off by really bad metaphors, think of the lemons as lemonade promising to quench your inner thirst.

Stoplight Prayers

Monica Furlong wrote in *Travelling In*,

> The Christian life can all be done on the spot. On this square
> foot of ground on which we stand we experience crucifixion and
> resurrection (if we are not so taken up with manipulating life that
> nothing can happen to us), and this is action, the action of love.
> It does not matter whether we do it in the solitude of a cell or in
> the New York subway. Only the moment matters. This is where
> God is.

How many times a day does each of us sigh when we see the light turn red
with the thought of being trapped for the next two or three minutes—or longer if
hoping to turn left? Multiply how many times a day this happens, times how many
times a week, times how many times a year. Conservatively, that's forty hours a year
essentially wasted.

Instead of fuming or texting or punching radio buttons—or, like some men
who somehow think they're invisible when picking their nose at a stoplight—think
instead of Thomas Merton and his legendary epiphany:

> In Louisville, at the corner of Fourth and Walnut, in the center
> of the shopping district, I was suddenly overwhelmed with the
> realization that I loved all those people, that they were mine and
> I theirs, that we could not be alien to one another even though
> we were total strangers. It was like waking from a dream of separ-
> ateness, of spurious self-isolation in a special world, the world of
> renunciation and supposed holiness. . . . This sense of liberation

from an illusory difference was such a relief and such a joy to me that I almost laughed out loud. . . . I have the immense joy of being man, a member of a race in which God Himself became incarnate. As if the sorrows and stupidities of the human condition could overwhelm me, now I realize what we all are. And if only everybody could realize this! But it cannot be explained. There is no way of telling people that they are all walking around shining like the sun.

Look at all those crossing the street, walking down the sidewalk, or stopped in cars around you, and think, *Yes, we're all shining like the sun. And I am one of you, and you are at one with me.* Stick a Post-It that simply says "Merton" as a reminder on your dashboard. Repeat "shining like the sun" for each person you see. And don't forget to include the man in the SUV. Today, Louisville's Fourth and Walnut is—fittingly, I think—Fourth and Muhammad Ali. It was Ali who could "float like a butterfly, sting like a bee," but who also believed that "service to others is the rent you pay for your room here on earth," a fitting companion to Merton's "realization that I loved all those people, that they were mine and I theirs, that we could not be alien to one another even though we were total strangers."

Other Prompts to Sneak Prayers without the Beads into Your Day

- Use the second hand on your smartphone's face to repeat a favorite or needed prayer phrase each second for thirty seconds while riding in an elevator or waiting for a light to change. If you're concerned about being conspicuous, don't be. Everyone else is looking at their phones too. Unfortunately.

Praying the Beads Without the Beads

- When scheduled for an MRI—everyone's favorite pastime—work *with* the machine instead of being terrified. Think of those awful beeps as prayer prompts of gratitude for the medical miracle you are experiencing. If you can't quite wrap your mind around gratitude, just pray Anne Lamott's phrase "Help. Thanks. Wow." Or maybe just "Help"? You can't move, of course, but keep count of the beeps with your toes and fingers.
- Many individual sports—tennis, pickle ball, racquetball, squash—are repetitive, muscle-memory opportunities for prayer.
- Video games and pinball machines work too. Just avoid violent ones.
- Weeding is a handy meditative opportunity. You'll even look as though you're praying, bowing in supplication. Count a prayer for each weed pulled, pile them up, and carry them like an offering to the compost. We're all spiritual compost ourselves.
- Folding laundry is a never-ending gift. Each fold of a towel can become a prayer. Again, carry the stack to the closet like an offering.

From the moment you fling back your bed covers in the morning, your day is already filled and waiting with objects and opportunities that can substitute for your beads when it's not convenient to stop and use them. Just think of these substitutions as prayers in action rather than repose.

Jesus and Tomatoes Coming Soon

Unsolicited prayers often sneak up and startle me in mid-activity.

The summer we spent in North Carolina, Jim and I stopped at one of the ubiquitous fresh-produce buildings that line the stretch of two-lane Highway 64 we traveled daily between Hendersonville and Brevard. We asked the two proprietors,

North Carolina versions of PBS's *Two Fat Ladies*, for their best tomatoes. One of the women laughed as she pointed to a basketful of unappealingly warped and bruise-colored tomatoes. We looked back at her, querulous. "Yep," she said, as she chose two of those scary-looking, over-heavy growths and plopped them into our hands. "They're Cherokee Purples, Honey. Take 'em home and try 'em. You'll be back."

Fixing dinner that night, I washed the tomatoes and, feeling like Abraham approaching Isaac, raised the knife rather high. They looked tough. But as the richly deep-red slices slowly fell apart from the knife, I was swept in a sensual rush to more than sixty years earlier in my grandmother's kitchen. I remembered the sun splashing through her kitchen window on the still life of tomatoes lined up fresh from the garden, the smell of the vine still clinging, the fierceness of the reds, the beads of salt releasing the musty scent of fecund earth. Eve, still naked, bit into that forbidden fruit, its burst of juice sliding down her chin and neck. I was nine years old again.

I was even aware of the phenomenon I think we've all experienced, of thinking in childhood that a grandparent's home seemed large and grand and then, years later, realizing it was only a normal-sized house. In that moment, though, my grandmother's kitchen was a palace of linoleum, and that parted tomato contained all the assumed magic of my childhood. I think I gasped a little, trying to stop time, understanding after several years David Craig's poem "Pentecost":

> What is this Holy Spirit?
> And what is it doing in the eggplant?

Jim and I made daily visits to the Fat Ladies. Each night for the next two weeks after dinner, I cleaned up while he hunkered in the cabin's basement methodically scraping each tomato seed from our plates onto laid-out, yellowing newspaper. We were familiar, too, having heard her in concert the year before, with Kate Campbell's ironically joyous song "Jesus and Tomatoes Coming Soon," based on a sign she'd seen one day near Asheville. We sang its refrain every day on the way to or from the Fat Ladies.

I didn't know that Jim had funneled all those dried seeds into a ziplock and carefully driven them home to his freezer, where they waited, silent and patient, or, two years later when we married, that he'd brought the ziplock of seeds from his old refrigerator to our new home. Because our own yard was torn up by construction and we had no garden, Jim presented my daughter with a handful of those seeds to plant without much expectation. She nurtured them for months like a firstborn. Her cut into that first tomato, which she presented to us with ceremony, was once again a moment of childhood magic. The Holy Spirit had been patient for three years.

And now I, and Abraham, and Eve, and my nine-year-old self wait each summer for that first Cherokee Purple from our garden, and I say, slicing into that first bite, *Oh, thank you, Holy Spirit.* Each year that first tomato is a prayer.

7
Homework: Life as a Set of Prayer Beads

Dante begins the *Inferno* with the mid-life acknowledgment that "In the middle of the journey of our life" he comes to himself in a dark wood, where the direct way seems lost. It is hard to speak of, Dante says, and the way ahead seems wild, harsh, and impenetrable. It is only with the appearance and guidance of the poet Virgil, and Dante's divine vision of his beloved Beatrice, that Dante finds his path on his journey. What Virgil teaches him is that the only way up is, in fact, the way down, down to the very last circle of hell before the ascent can begin.

Dante's use of the term "dark wood" has appeared throughout the centuries in other tales, and the same image has featured in other myths, including stories of quest for the Grail. In the modern world it was borrowed by the psychoanalyst Carl Jung and Jungian analysts—notably James Hollis, who brought the term to popular consciousness. Even the musical *Into the Woods* is based on the concept.

Dante's experience of being lost is a situation that includes us all. And often, hell looks very modern indeed, even sometimes with cheap sheets. I know because, like many others, I have been there and can report back.

"Well, I think it's time we nipped this in the bud," my psychologist Kip said. I had begun seeing Kip when my marriage was unraveling and, increasingly, had

begun having panic attacks. I had paged him from my kitchen, where without warning while writing out a grocery list for a dinner party I was hosting two nights later, a panic attack began.

At the time little medically was known about panic attacks. They were often accompanied by a rush to a hospital with a diagnosis of stroke or cardiac arrest. My first attack happened out of the blue in a grocery checkout line. Gripping my cart's handle, I gradually became aware that I couldn't breathe. My arms and legs felt as though they were disembodied, and I was convinced I was becoming irretrievably crazy, about to be flung as jagged shrapnel to circle in orbit, trapped, for oblivion. My heart, as though on a loud speaker, skipped beats and pounded in my ears, filling my head with enormous pressure. Convinced I was having a heart attack or stroke, I gasped in heaves, grasping for air.

I had no reference frame for this experience. When you scrape your knee, when you hit your elbow—or even break a bone—you know the level of pain to expect. And when it's over, it's over. The reality of a full-blown anxiety attack hits you without warning, however; the fear does not recede but increases. The dread of recurring ones is substantial and terrifying. You don't know you're having one until, too late, it is already occurring. Time slows, the landscape reels. Your fear smells like a feral animal.

Over the next few weeks wherever I happened to be when an attack occurred became off-limits. The fear of a recurrence—at any one of an increasing number of stores or in an elevator—quickly shrank what some internal, primitive animal antennae marked as the perimeter of my safe universe. I, who only a few years earlier had hitchhiked through seven European countries and, without a second thought, through the Alps in the middle of a blizzard in a truck hauling sheep, could not now imagine driving across a short, nondescript city bridge. My house was the one place I felt safe, the one haven I knew I could count on.

And now it had happened. Standing in my kitchen, my hand shook trying to dial Kip's pager number. When it beeped, I slammed my phone number into his pager.

"Yep, we need to nip this in the bud," Kip said again. "Meet me at the hospital, and we'll take care of this."

In my ignorance and haughtiness I had discounted Kip. He was too young—he looked as though he'd just walked off a high school baseball diamond; his accent was too Southern; he wore the wrong kind of shoes. He could not possibly have anything worth saying to me. Now, however, he was my lifeline.

We met at the hospital and walked down the hall and through a heavy industrial door that closed with a commanding swoosh and an echoing click as it locked automatically. I was left at the nurses' station with my overnight bag.

"This here's all you brought?" the plus-sized nurse in blue scrubs asked as she opened my bag and started emptying each item onto the counter.

"Uh, yeah, it's just for the weekend," I said, breathing lightly.

Her eyebrows rose, lips tightened.

"Well, you can't have this," she snorted, lifting my razor out of the bag and plunking it against the Formica counter. "Or these!" she said, holding up a small glass bottle of perfume—twirling it to read the label—and a narrow crocodile belt I wore with my jeans.

"But why not?" I was growing alarmed.

"Because you might try to slit your wrists or your neck or hang yourself. We gotta protect you from yourself!" And she scooped the rest of the items back into my suitcase and snapped the locks with finality. "Here you go, honey. It's yours now," she said, sliding my suitcase across the counter toward me. Her nails were bitten off at the quicks.

I can still remember this moment and the snap of the suitcase locks. I knew I was in a psychiatric unit and I had heard the hissing pneumatic lock of the door echoing down the concrete-block hallway, but it wasn't until that moment that I felt the icy frisson of hairs standing up across the back of my neck like a trapped animal's. As an aide walked me down a long, shadowed hallway to show me to my room, I thought of the inscription over Dante's gate to hell: "Abandon hope, all ye who enter here."

That night the demons I'd unknowingly controlled for so many years unleashed themselves, a tsunami of depression and despair and panic. The attacks came one after another. A nurse sat across from my bed, leaning toward me from a chair, and held my hands. She looked unwavering into my eyes darting in terror, and told me quietly and evenly to breathe deeply and slowly. She gave me a shot. As I drifted to sleep in the anonymous, institutional room under the cheap, thin bedspread, I said goodbye to the world I'd known for forty years.

I became a guinea pig. Because my reaction to any therapeutic drugs was an unknown, a hit-and-miss barrage of different drugs exploded in my body. I was simultaneously exhausted and wired. Nothing worked. My blood pressure zoomed out of control. I remember the horrified look on the doctor's face as I tried at one point to describe the fluorescent orange spikes that registered like a vivid EKG printout across my mind's eye when I spoke. Trying to see through the glaring, frantic static as I spoke was frustrating and alarming. I reached forward, trying to touch the fluorescent spikes, but the moving image was not external, only in my head. The doctor left the room abruptly, a fixed expression on her face, and came back quickly, armed with an unnamed pill.

For the next several days I could not control my legs easily and had to lean against the wall for support and balance as I walked down the hall. Likewise, whenever I had a phone call on the communal wall phone, I lacked the energy to stand up straight and—the phone cord not long enough to reach the floor—had to hug the wall with the phone propped against my shoulder. Conversations were tiring and nonsensical. Words seemed to jerk out of my mouth.

I was literally locked into this unit. Other patients could sign out to go outside during the day, but for my first two weeks I was not allowed to leave the unit. And I didn't want to leave. I didn't look out of windows; even the distant, faint sound of trucks rushing along a nearby expressway filled me with ungrounded dread. The minutiae of the normal, commonplace world was too threatening. I stayed exhausted from hair-trigger responses to the insignificant. Even the shower was threatening and claustrophobic.

Meals were obstacles. Walking down the cafeteria line was like passing through a gauntlet. The food repulsed me; the smell of heated industrial plastic trays and worn plastic plates, still damp from the dishwasher, was nauseating. I sat at random tables simply staring at my tray. Peoples' conversations made no sense, and everyone seemed to talk in jarring, loud voices. The lighting was too harsh. People rising from their chairs loomed out of perspective and startled me. Although known to cuss as imaginatively as any sailor, I found the sound of any shouted cuss word offensive, physically abrasive. I began to lose weight rapidly.

After weeks of becoming progressively sicker, all I knew was that, very simply, I wanted to die. I don't know which carried more lethal weight: the social and personal stigma of being in a psychiatric hospital, my inability to accept my vulnerability and loss of self, the various pills' side effects, or my resistance to letting the medicine work. I had failed. I was not worthy of getting well.

Daily group therapy was a requisite. I condescended. My resistance to the ideas of needing help and of help coming from the group process was formidable. These people I sat around in a circle with every day were not, I believed, acceptable. They were not my people. A tight, smug me thought I was better than they were: I had studied and traveled in Europe for two years, I had been chairman of an English department and instructor at two community colleges, and I had just illustrated and written a cookbook. I knew "important" people in the city. I clung desperately to these illegitimate values.

I had always enjoyed analyzing and critiquing problems; I lived in my head, so I was comfortable telling the therapy group members what was wrong with each of them. It was not all right, however, for anyone to call me out. I would sit in tight, puffed-up anger thinking the stupid session was paying for one more tire on Kip's Porsche.

My eight-and-a-half weeks were punctuated, however, with moments of kindness and occasional humor. A couple of days after arriving, I walked into my room, and sitting on the chest of drawers in the dreary January light was an immense arrangement of spring flowers sent by my friend Barbara. Its colors—and the thought that she would treat my hospitalization like any other hospitalization, for a broken leg or childbirth—ripped through my shroud of stigma like fierce sunshine. I sat on my bed and wept. They were the only flowers I received in more than eight weeks. I even wonder today, many "enlightened" years later, how many people send flowers to friends in a psychiatric unit.

My aunt and uncle, Sis and Ed, who lived in the country outside a small Southern town, called me most nights after early dinner, chatting nonchalantly, just to "check in," telling me each night, "It's all right, honey, you're going to be just fine, just fine. We just wanted to say 'hi.'" Although standing at the phone and carrying on a conversation took such effort, my gratitude at their easy conversation and reassurance continues to be one of my more important life lessons: Even if you don't send flowers, show up. Just show up in some way. And the words don't matter.

I was discharged after five-and-a-half weeks with ineffective medication, and my depression quickly spread and flooded, a river breaching a levee. I have little memory of this time, only of the increasing thoughts of suicide as the sole remedy for the emotional and physical pain stalking my hours.

My depression was not just an emotional, mental pain; it pinned me to the bed exhausted and withering. Writhing, black, prehistoric lizards from a tarry pit—scaly tongues flicking and wrapping around my lungs, dirty claws digging into my ribs— gorged on my heart and stomach, circling for the best attack, leaving flayed ends of jagged flesh as they consumed me from the inside out. I lay in bed sapped, paralyzed by their weight, sorting through different ways of killing myself. Driving off the bridge at full speed became my choice. A far-off flicker of reason registered feebly that I was dangerously sick when I knew I didn't care what my death would do to my three-, four-, and eleven-year olds.

Ethel, who had worked with my parents for almost thirty years, alternated with my mother in helping with the children. She came one morning, realized my condition, and called my mother, who came and drove me to the doctor's office. I was not allowed to leave the office, my mother was sent back to my house to pack a bag, and I was driven back to the hospital, where I was put on Suicide Watch, a burly aide planted in a chair in the doorway of my room.

I was forced again to go to group therapy, where I sat silent and motionless, the weight of depression squeezing and shriveling my breath. The third day the therapist suddenly stopped and made me get on the floor. I was made to crawl to each person's chair, stopping in front of each one in the circle to say one reason not to kill myself. The humiliation was intense.

Later I was stunned by the paradox that in humbling myself, kneeling before each of these once-dismissed fellow patients, I was in fact crawling toward healing. It was

an epiphany, and I think I caught a glimpse of Jesus outside the door giving a high-five to a passing aide. I have since learned that my recognition of truth most often occurs long after the fact. I seem to learn only after God has left the building, as we are reminded in Exodus when Yahweh and Moses have a little chat. I have come to know that humiliation often can be the beginning of humility. And gratitude.

Coincidentally, and luckily, the doctor tried one more antidepressant, a rarely used early form of medication. It slowly began to work. I felt like a swimmer held under canyons of deep, dark water too long slowly being pulled to the surface, light, and air. I gasped at new life.

Although I was far from healed, it was time to go home. Kip knew better than I the long road that lay ahead for me. "We've tried every medication available, Suzanne. There isn't anything left—except to give God a chance," were his last stunning words to me before I left the hospital. I found it startling to hear a psychologist give blatant theological advice. I had no idea who "God" was. Certainly there had been no burning bushes or voice from a cloud during all this time, and praying was not a practice I understood or entertained. Years earlier I had ignorantly told my friend John, who'd invited my husband and me to his church, that I couldn't possibly go, that I would feel like a hypocrite unless I had a Saul-on-the-road-to-Damascus experience. He quietly replied, "But that's what the Episcopal Church does, Suzanne. It takes you wherever you are."

I remembered his words after Kip discharged me and, although without any thought of expectation or meaning or belief at the time, began taking my three children to church.

I also had to see Kip for follow-up sessions for eight weeks after leaving the hospital. It was still difficult for me to drive far from home—fire-spitting dragons still patrolled the expressway lying in wait for me—but I made it each week. During one session I asked him why, weeks earlier during my inpatient stay, my patient notebook containing all the professional notes about me had disappeared from the nurses' station. I had asked the nurse where it was so I could sign out to walk to the lake. "They're discussing you in staff meeting," the nurse had said curtly." I had been furious at what I thought was the violation of my privacy. And now I was curious to hear Kip's response.

"Well," he said, clearing his throat, "you were the most depressed patient I'd ever treated." He paused, gauging my reaction, and looked me in the eye. "We didn't think you were going to make it."

And then, after a short silence, we both smiled.

Slowly, over many months during which I continued to feel like an outcast, a social misfit, unable to concentrate or read or even put together two meaningful sentences, I found myself slowly practicing a new confidence.

Rehab is never speedy or cheap, whether one is talking about alcohol, drugs, psychiatry, hip replacement, or houses. The process is never a straight line; sacrifice is a given. Surprises and expense—whether emotional or for housing construction materials and labor—are guaranteed. It is physically exhausting and demonstrably rewarding. I enjoy the irony that, of the several different occupations I have had since leaving the hospital and returning to the world, one of the more fulfilling has been as a contractor rehabbing derelict, early twentieth-century cottages. I buy, gut, redesign, and renovate homes worn down by age and misuse, and retain the good bones and architectural integrity while reconstructing the living space. My crew, who over the years have become my second family, and I work hard creating new life, just as in the hospital I learned the necessities of rehabbing parts of myself, throwing out the dead and useless—as difficult as some of those rotting boards are to pull out, nail by nail—admiring the grain of old wood worth saving, and always checking the beams and foundation before tearing out a wall.

And, as trite as it is to say, we are all, of course, rehabs. Every moment. Every day. Even when we seem to be stuck out in some endless, parched desert, our hearts and souls cracking and dying of thirst, we're handed the gift of starting over. Failure simply means an opportunity to begin again. We get to wrench out those old, rusted nails we worked so hard to hammer in crookedly, pull out the warped boards, and try once more to hammer a straighter nail. Every day.

I no longer hitch rides through Alpine blizzards as I did in my twenties; my journeys now are usually internal, marked by detour signs, green lights, and amazement. I still occasionally spot dragons silhouetted against the horizon of the expressway, but most are toothless and tired-looking, fires spent. They remind me, though, of Didion's advice "to keep on nodding terms with the people we used to be." So now I swaddle and cradle all those selves, many still spitting a need for control—willful, stubborn, scratching and muddied, scraping up the mined hillside of ignorance—and tote them over my shoulder stuffed in a patched and threadbare bag. They're still noisy and unruly but now fairly light baggage and, shifting their weight, I sing, slightly off-key, to them all, *Yes, thank you, thank you, yes*. There are no regrets.

Gratitude is all.

In different ways and to varying degrees we each wander from the "right" path, most often recognizing ourselves lost in the dark woods at midpoint between the first and second halves of life. It is only in learning from the often painful lessons of darkness that we are able to move into our more authentic selves. On the other side of those woods, we often find that wisdom and gratitude are waiting to open their wings inside us and lift us off the ground.

Although saying "Life is a set of prayer beads" makes me feel like a bumper sticker, or Forrest Gump and his box of chocolates, our lives are indeed living rosaries, regardless of whatever it is we happen to believe—or not believe—about religion and the Spirit.

The beads of a rosary are like Jungian "stepping stones"—an unintentional but apt reference to the pebbled Psalms of the original Desert Fathers. Like the decades of a Catholic rosary or twenty-eight Weeks or lesser beads of Protestant prayer beads, we are made of a variety of experiences and people that mark the metaphorical "decades," "weeks," or "seasons" of our lives. Each memorable experience or person is a stepping stone to who we become. It is interesting to note that Bill Wilson, cofounder of AA who created the Twelve-Step Movement, even named his historic-register home Stepping Stones after the practices that have brought millions to wholeness.

Nineteenth-century theologian and Massachusetts bishop Phillips Brooks, when asked what made him a Christian, famously paused and said, "I think I am a Christian because of my aunt who lives in Teaneck, New Jersey." We are our stories. We become who we are because of our relationships—relationships with other people, with nature, with our God. And the "truths" of these relationships always speak to us through stories, not lecturing. Jesus knew this certainly. We've wrestled with his stories, his parables, for more than two thousand years.

In the next chapter we'll wrestle with your Cruciform beads—those experiences of "crucifixion" that indelibly define who we have been, are, and will become. Now, however, this is your homework: Brainstorm making a list—chronologically or higgledy-piggeldy—of people and events that have in some way influenced the "you" of you. You can do it all in one sitting or break it up into several attempts. You might balk at first but, as Jenny Lawson gratefully learned from fellow writer and friend Neil Gaiman in the midst of crippling anxiety and depression, "just pretend you're good at it." Pencil to paper is all that matters right now.

What you'll learn, I think, is that once you begin, events will flood your awareness so quickly—and with surprise of memory!—that you can't jot experiences down quickly enough. Some of these will be happy moments; some, of course, not quite so. But take time to rummage around in the memory of each one, and approach each from the sneaky periphery of what it now in retrospect might teach you. Leave the list lying around handily with pen or pencil, or start a document and leave it open on your computer desktop—though, if you have a sixteen-year-old or inquisitive mate, you might want to keep it somewhere discrete. Don't worry about coming up with twenty-eight "beads" of neat ideas. And, for heaven's sake, don't think they are supposed to make you look impressive, even to yourself. Start small. Be honest.

Write about a family member or close friend and about experiences—even ones that someone else might dismiss or be unaware of—that seem to have guided your life. For instance, I've written about experiences while working for hospice that have continued long after the events themselves to affect my thinking and actions toward others as well as my views about dying. I've written about my unintentional creation

of a "moveable Eucharist" with Diet Coke and peanut-butter crackers while ringing the bell every year for the Salvation Army and meeting those who donate—one of whom, in worn pink house slippers, pulled out a wrinkled dollar and told me, "Honey, just because I have to be on food stamps don't mean I don't know how important it is to give!" I've realized the importance, while looking at the morning paper's lineup of convicted fugitives' defiant mug shots of praying for these men and women as well as for their victims. Each morning I look past their defiant mug shot scowls and create new possibilities in life for them in my mind. This exercise has made me acutely aware that we are called to pray for our "enemies," a most difficult but profound demand that we so easily disregard. I've also written about experiences when I've betrayed friendships and lied to protect my ego. The range of these memories combine in defining me to myself.

One memory I've written about that has been a continuing sense of both awe and joy was an experience while living in Europe in my twenties. My friend Jonathan and I were hitchhiking back to Florence from Sicily, determined to visit Le Corbusier's architecturally mythic Chapelle Notre Dame du Haut in Ronchamp, France. We rode through the night in the cab of a truck of sheep with a driver crossing the Alps in a snowstorm. Our world became a moonless black except for the swirling snow caught in the truck's headlights. Suddenly the driver came to a stop at a mountaintop crossroad and told us in a mixture of French and Italian that this was the end of our ride, that he had to turn off.

Nothing existed but mountain, snow, biting cold, and black sky. Using cigarette lighters, we read the small crossroad's sign that indicated with a hand-carved arrow a children's summer retreat two kilometers across the forested darkness. With the light of the snow guiding us, we found the sleeping camp, and Jonathan broke a pane in the glass door. Freezing, and in the dark, we maneuvered around stacked farm tables and benches until we came to a bare, dead-end room and wrapped up, exhausted, in sleeping bags.

The next morning, breaths creating clouds of cold, we woke to the sound of tinkling bells, blinding snow, and the tap of hooves. We were lying seven feet under the ceiling, a huge glass skylight that grew out of the side of the mountain. The morning sun burned drifts of steam from the glass and shot darting prisms around the room like lasers. Through the blinding glare we saw a goat, then another, then ten goats standing above our heads on the glass, their bells clanging, hooves tapping, making the morning a cacophony of greeting and celebration as they nosed through the snow, tap-dancing on the glass above our heads. This image of feeling like being there when God created light has followed me for my lifetime.

Remember that, as your list grows, you can cross out people or experiences that don't seem as formative as they might have when you first thought of them. Draw arrows and asterisks when necessary; doodle along the sides of the page while thinking. Messy or OCD, it's up to you. No one else will see this.

Next, take a sheet of computer paper and fill it with a simple drawing of a set of Protestant prayer beads. Remember this is not art. Shading and perspective are not issues. Just draw twenty-eight bumps that sort of look like circles of the same size.

When you think you are at a stopping place, arrange the events in chronological order, and label each of the Weeks circles with an experience, beginning on the bottom right and circling up to the left, skipping the Cruciform circles.

Keep this sheet safe. You'll need it in the next chapter.

You are holding your life in your hands. Be gentle.

8
The Cruciform Beads of Life

The Cruciform beads of a rosary offer opportunities for us to reflect on those profound experiences that force us to "die" to our old self in order to more authentically become our true selves. They signify both crucifixion and resurrection. And, needless to say, they are usually painful.

Who wants to give up the old-shoe comfort of the expected—even when it is destructive and, even after many repetitions, has never worked as a solution? Ask any recovering addict. No one wants his ego crucified. "What the ego (False Self) hates and fears more than anything else," Rohr reminds us in *Immortal Diamond*, "is change. It will think up a thousand other things to be concerned about or be moralistic about—anything rather than giving up 'who I think I am' and 'who I need to be to look good.'"

Each event that we replay and replay is like squeezing a prayer bead as a plea. Often, bottom line, these experiences involve needed forgiveness, both of others and of ourselves. Although joy can be the source of transformation, it's iffy; more often joy is the discovery only after we have painfully shed that old snakeskin self.

Your Instructions

The format is a continuation of the exercise you began in the previous chapter with the Weeks beads. This could be an effective exercise for a book club or church group, or it could serve as the focus of a weekend retreat. It is often the basis for workshops like the Jungian-based Progoff Intensive Journal Program. Investigate whether any workshop similar to the Progoff is or could be offered in your area.

If winging it alone, get your drawing of a set of prayer beads on which you've labeled the Weeks beads of your life and, discerning over a period of time who you've been at different points and who you are now, label each of the Cruciform beads with an experience that has marked your more authentic identity. This is not a five-minute, one-sitting exercise! You can mark out, erase, draw arrows, have subplots, move a Cruciform onto one of the Weeks beads—and vice versa. Keep the sheet handy for labeling more experiences, both lesser and major, as you later think of them.

Next, choose one of the experiences and journal about it on separate sheets. If part of a group, you can choose to share or not. Continue to journal about your beads depending on your timeframe and interest. You might decide to choose a new one to write about once a week—for instance, every Thursday morning at 6:00— and let your subconscious work for you during the week until it's time for you to write.

One of the Cruciform beads I've written about is how my passion for fly-fishing has woven through my years. Repeatedly I have learned that standing in a river, anchored against the current, and casting a fly line is a process that can heal when other more traditional means fail. Casting is itself a body prayer. Time ceases; I'm anchored in silence, the kind of silence necessary for me to hear. Fishing is recreation but it is also wrapped into the mystery of re-creation. I have fished through litanies of grief—over the deaths of a marriage, my father, a lover, my mother, and my only brother, Jeff, with whom I fished often on many rivers, and who taught me both the literal and spiritual meaning of catch and release.

I've fished more than twenty rivers from Oregon to North Carolina through a litany of deaths, yes, but these years are also layered with humor and deep friendships. The latest chapters took place a few years ago, beginning when my three children, my fly-fishing son-in-law, and my new grandchild, Kate, and I were in Montana.

Each afternoon from a window we'd watch a bear lumber across the low boulders joining two trout streams behind the house and disappear into the dense forest up the mountain. One afternoon, without warning, I called everyone to the stream. We stood in sweaters and old jeans holding hands, balanced on the rocks. With apologies to the Book of Common Prayer, I began: "Kate, we stand here, surrounded by angels known and unknown, in the path of the bear, on rocks older than we can dream about, beside the waters of trout from which we all once came, to welcome you to this world. We stand here to wish you an inquiring and discerning heart, the courage to will and to persevere, a spirit to know and to love, and the gift of joy and wonder. And you, we know, have come to teach us about unconditional love. May we learn our lesson well."

And I reached into the pocket of my jeans, pulled out a battered measuring cup from the kitchen, dipped it into the trout stream, and baptized my grandchild.

Two years later I baptized my grandson Otto, Kate's brother, in that same trout stream. When my son, Walker, and his wife, Bailey, had their first child, Charles, they wanted him baptized not in Montana but on their own land—land in the foothills of the Monteagle Mountain range that has been in Bailey's family for eight generations—in the ageless spring that gathers in a bouldered pool behind their house. Four generations of family held hands as we welcomed Charles to our world, and I handed the antique silver cup to his granddad Mike, Bailey's father, who gently dipped the cup into the stream and welcomed Charles with the primal water of unconditional love.

Baby Hollan will be next. And may they all, these beads in the lineage of my life, become lovers of the light that flows from rivers. May they know the deep joy of communion offered there. And may they know and sing with that Spirit that often dances on the end of a fly line.

I have their first rods picked out.

Cruciform experiences can also balance on that thin line that separates comedy and tragedy. I, for instance, have written about the trauma of my boyfriend pointing out loudly, in a very crowded, elbow-to-elbow restaurant waiting line, that I had a white chin hair—"It's about an inch long," he announced—sticking out under my chin. "Do you want me to pull it for you?" he asked. This experience was one of the more excruciating ones of my life. But I also remember snorting my iced tea afterward at lunch from laughing so hard. And then I married him.

Sometimes Cruciform experiences can border the physically literal. The latest "bead" I've written about is my recent "widow maker" heart attack, a truly Cruciform experience. I recounted the semi-conscious feeling of riding in the tinny ambulance as though over WWI trenches and minefields and thinking the Holy Spirit, in cowboy boots and long hair flying in the wind, was riding a Harley Davidson beside us. I hazily thought he must have to shop at Goodwill because of all the costume changes demanded by his activities. I then imagined him in scrubs slipping into the OR as the doctor threaded a tube from my thigh up and into my heart. I watched the monitor as blood vessels danced and twirled—"like pole dancers!" I remember exclaiming to the stunned doctor, who quickly put me to sleep.

The next morning the doctor came to my room and said, "Mrs. Henley, I've come to tell you that you need to know there's no scientific explanation why you're still alive." I just stared at him, stunned. "Obviously, someone thinks you have unfinished business."

I thought of this book half-finished and thought, *No, you weren't saved so you could finish a silly book, for heaven's sake. There's always unfinished business in anyone's life. You just had a damn good cardiology interventionist.*

Occasionally, though, in quiet moments I hold this conundrum up to the light and turn it slowly. And whatever the mystery is, I'm grateful.

I wrote about my new practices in church as a result of my stent. When saying the Lord's Prayer, I now place my hand over my heart and stent with the words "who art in heaven, hallowed be thy name. Thy kingdom come, thy will be done, on earth as it is in heaven." Any observers probably think I'm confused and think I'm reciting the Pledge of Allegiance, which in a way I am: an allegiance to my belief that I create heaven here and now, unconcerned about later. It's the treasure I store up in my heart.

My stent is now a metaphorical portal reminding me to keep my often hard, judgmental, and controlling heart open to the hallowing power of love and the inexplicable mystery offered us.

Years ago, making sure I looked convincingly solemn, I enjoyed walking slowly down the aisle to the altar rail for communion as though in a royal procession. I'd wonder if my panty line showed and, when kneeling, whether

a sticker was still on the bottom of my shoes, announcing its discount price to the congregation.

Metaphors, though, have saved me from my ignorance. The words "do this in remembrance of me" now speak resoundingly. At the altar I sink down on my knees, arms outstretched, to ask that the universal Christ in me—that has been shattered and misguided and dismembered—be "re-membered," pounded back together again and committed for the coming week in my heart, a heart I've seen and, with awe, watched dance. I often forget the way to dance, to practice love. I have to be reminded. I have to be re-membered. Over and over.

Now on a double portion of blood thinner, if I even unknowingly brush against anything, I immediately bruise. My wrists and forearms stay encircled by large purple splotches of varying hues at any given time; I nick and bleed and scar easily. These splotches do not hurt; they just look dreadful. I tell friends I hope that people think Jim and I are into vigorous bondage rather than defining me as old and frail.

I choose to think these marks are gifts from the blood of my heart—both literally and metaphorically true—visible reminders, along with my stent: my Jacob's wounds, signs I have wrestled with my angel. And, yes, I will limp like Jacob for the rest of this life, but I'll also dance.

There is an addition to this story. I continued to be intrigued why I insisted on imagining the Holy Spirit garbed in black leather on a Harley. One Saturday not long ago, Jim and I headed to The Cupboard, the most notable of Memphis's "meat+three" restaurants, for lunch. It is large and very popular with a diversity of customers, all drawn to traditional Southern cooking marked by memories of childhood.

We pulled into the parking lot and, parked right at the front door, was a very large, chromed and white Harley, hunkering at an angled slant on its kickstand. Jim of course knew before I said anything what my plan was: Find the owner and engage him in a conversation about my Holy Spirit. Jim's sigh told me what he thought.

We sat and ordered. I had no trouble spotting the probable owners, a man and woman in noticeably Harley gear. He had a bandana tied around his head and reflective sunglasses; she wore Harley boots. I noticed when they had finished their meal and rose from their table. Jim, halfway through his lunch, barely rolled his eyes as I threw down my napkin and stood up. "I'll see you at checkout," I said.

As the couple passed me by the door after paying, I took a breath and squeaked, "Do you mind if I ask you a couple of questions? I'm not crazy, but you'll probably think I am." They tilted their heads invitingly, so I launched in: "I write, and I need to know why I have this nagging image of the Holy Spirit riding a Harley. Can you tell me why I think he should be on a Harley?"

The man didn't miss a beat. "The sound, of course the sound is the first reason," he said and immediately started explaining mid-century, Midwestern hay-baling engines as the Harley's precursor. The technicalities about pistons and rods continued, and his voice rose with his excitement. The woman with him stood patiently listening. And I, technically challenged, listened, fascinated, realizing this was a subject deeply meaningful to him, even if it was way too much seemingly irrelevant information to me.

And then he paused and said, "Do you mind if we tell you our Holy Spirit stories?"

We were strangers standing in a very crowded restaurant as the mid-day crowd and waiters rushed by us back and forth, and he said, "We've come from North Carolina, and this is probably the last trip on our bucket list. My wife, Glenda, here has terminal cancer, breast cancer that's spread to her lungs and bones. We're headed to the Grand Canyon. One day, taking Glenda to chemo as usual, I leaned down in my chair and prayed. No one was around. It was very quiet. And then I heard footsteps, and then a hand pressing on my shoulder, and then a voice in my ear saying, "She will be well."

Tears were running down the cheeks of this former long-distance truck driver, a retired policeman. Glenda's eyes glistened, and she touched his arm and said, "Tell her about the other time."

"Well," he said, "she was a detention officer in a woman's prison, but she's retired, too, because she can't be around people now 'cause her immune system is so compromised. On this day I'm talking about she had four prisoners, two upstairs in cells and two downstairs. She had to check on them every thirty minutes and write a report. Well, she finished her rounds and was writing the report downstairs at her desk when she heard a noise upstairs. Ordinarily she wouldn't have given it a thought—she'd finished her work—but for some reason she painfully climbed back upstairs. She found the woman hanging from a sheet she'd strung over a light fixture. She'd jumped off the toilet and was quietly and slowly swinging. Frail little Glenda here climbed up on the toilet seat and held the woman up in the air for all the minutes it took until someone else could get there to help."

I stood there with about seventeen emotions running up my arms and through my heart and down my legs. Saying anything would have diminished the moment. We simply rested in this shimmering moment, hugged, and walked out together into the 99-degree heat, standing on the unforgiving asphalt by their magnificent, spotlessly white touring bike. We hugged again, they strapped on their helmets, and we all waved as they kicked that reverberating engine into gear, its throbbing engine echoing at idle before they accelerated, leaning into their broad arc onto Union Avenue, off on their 4,000-mile journey, a journey obviously of more than miles.

We have all, like Abraham, entertained angels unaware. It didn't just happen in stories of tents in a desert three thousand years ago on the other side of the world. It can happen any day, over dishes of turnip greens and sweet potatoes, or standing on blazing asphalt in the middle of a city.

I've decided my fascination with the Harley probably has to do with freedom, a variation of that illusory freedom created during the opening credits of the quintessential Harley movie, *Easy Rider*. The Holy Spirit, though, rides in to give us, I think, the promise of real freedom, freedom from whatever has hog-tied our souls. That day, as I imagined Him accelerating down Union to catch up with Gifford and Glenda on their cross-country trip, I knew He didn't need to make a stop at Goodwill first. He already had the right outfit for the trip.

As you define the experiences of your own Cruciform beads, may the Holy Spirit ride with you!

And, again, remember your sheet might become wrinkled and messy looking—like many of us and our lives—but also remember you are holding your life in your hands. Handle it gently.

9
The Crucible

Glass—which both occurs naturally as obsidian volcanic ash and is one of our oldest man-created materials—is made by firing silica (basically sand, one of earth's most ancient elements) up to 4,000 degrees Fahrenheit. This has been the process since glass-making was discovered more than 3,500 years ago in Mesopotamia. Beads from that period are the oldest known glass objects and are examples of some of the earliest examples of sacramental art.

My initially reluctant introduction to prayer beads began with an equally reluctant introduction to glasswork. I began working in a medium called *fused* or *warm* glass as a deferred favor to a major donor at the college where I was director of development. She was a glass artist, and one day in my office I complimented a piece of work she brought to the college. She invited me to come to her studio and learn basic techniques. I was not at all interested but, after she had invited me five or six times over a period of two months, became embarrassed and felt professionally compelled to give an evening to the experience. Contrary to my long-suffering expectations, the experience "took," and now I create large, glass bas-relief and mosaic wall pieces for private, corporate, and nonprofit organization commissions, as well as bas-relief wall tiles for kitchens and baths, cabinet and drawer pulls, jewelry, crosses, and bowls and platters. Beads are often integral in these pieces.

From 36-inch heavy sheets of different colors of glass, I cut designs and layer them on other designs—sometimes five or seven layers thick—and fire them in one of two kilns in my basement. One of the kilns is a five-foot-long oblong shape—I call it "the coffin"—used for large work or for firing many different smaller pieces at the same time. The smaller kiln is round and eighteen inches in diameter. A firing—depending on the size and thickness of the layers—can take between twelve and twenty four hours; the temperature is programmed to increase at different, proscibed intervals to usually 1,450 degrees and is held there for varying lengths of time, again depending on size and depth.

During a firing, glass becomes molten and is transformed into a new creation. Glass never completely cools; it is a "frozen liquid," an amorphous solid like us—human *becomings* rather than finished human beings. This is often the process of prayer, that we are transformed during the process and come out of the experience new. To me, both these processes, glass firings and prayer, are crucibles.

I usually fire during the night, and there have been times when I lie in my bed in my 100-year-old house with the heavy, ancient beams of the basement over the kilns, and wonder what inferno could be sparked by those kilns. There have also been dark nights of the soul when I have lain seemingly nailed to my bed by the ancient beams of crucifying depression and despair, captive in the crucible of a spiritual inferno. Mythologist Joseph Campbell reminds us that "the problem with hell is that the fires don't consume you. The fires of transformation do," but also that "love informs the whole universe, right down into the abyss of hell." If we're lucky, we can open the top of the kiln of our soul and find we are new.

The physics of the firing process is fascinating—particuarly so because apparently I'm incapable of understanding it. For some reason I occasionally think I can charm and defy these physical laws, and time after time I've discovered it usually doesn't work.

I can push and cajole, but only up to a point. Opening the top of the kiln with childlike anticipation after a firing is like opening a Christmas present. Often the result is more than satisfactory but, occasionally, because I do try to one-up physics, the result can seem tragic. *Well*, I think, *I've shot myself in the foot once again. When will I learn?*

I've wasted much time and money—glass is a very expensive medium to work in—but, conversely, like much else in life, I often have found that the challenge of seeming tragedy can produce insight and a result more exciting than the original. I realize this sounds a bit like a Pinterest quote, but when it works, it is a gift.

One of the best corners of my life was a commission I received for creating six months of work in glass for the Memphis area's first residential hospice, the Baptist Reynolds Hospice House: a six-foot cross for the chapel; a nine-foot-long mosaic wall triptych recognizing major donors; six large glass and copper wall plaques identifying common rooms; and twenty-four wood-backed, arched room-donor plaques hung outside each patient door, lining both sides of the hallway of patient rooms. I also made one hundred donor thank-you pieces on stands.

The major-donor mosaic wall triptych contains more than eleven thousand hand-cut, 24-karat-gold-backed pieces of glass depicting a swoop of the Holy Spirit moving across the piece, and is accented by one hundred many-layered decorative mosaics, which lend a sense of texture and depth. The sun changing in the room plays across the tiles, creating a dance of light, and makes the swoop of the Spirit seem to move and hover.

While my helpers Robert and Cedric and I were working on the piece—filling up every inch of space in my dining room for several months, using my eight-foot-long dining table as the base for the mosaic's plywood backing—more than one hundred people, touched in some way by the mystery and holiness of death, came to my house, each like a pilgrim with a private message. As word spread they came one at a time, in pairs, in families, from friends and children of friends and friends of friends to hospital and hospice employees. Each chose one of the decorated tiles on the table, I showed them an appropriate empty space on the board that backed the piece, on which they wrote their message—I was always careful not to read what they wrote—and then they sealed the space with their chosen tile.

As the sun in that hospice common room moves, it not only plays across the glass but gathers all those hidden, secret messages into its light as moving prayers. Most people who walk by the triptych probably have no idea they are part of this dance of prayer—or that they themselves are dancing prayers too.

The cross in the chapel is six feet high and, in some places, is seven layers thick with decoration and definition. I was terrified while firing the pieces that eventually would fit together and be anchored on a six-foot-long, six-inch by six-inch wooden-base cross constructed by Clyde, a carpenter who had worked with me daily over the years during the renovations of nine houses. I have an indelible image of Clyde arriving at my house with that large, rough wooden cross sticking out of the back of his Dodge Ram (he didn't arrive on a colt or donkey). He must have caused double-takes as he drove down the commercial and residential streets to my house with a rough cross sticking up in the back of his pickup. The most memorable image I have, though, is of him carefully lifting that cross out of his truck, pulling down his baseball cap—it was no crown of thorns—and hoisting the heavy cross on his back to carry it up my uneven, antique-brick front walk and steps. Holding open my front door as he climbed each step, one at a time—carefully and purposefully planting each boot flat-footed for balance—I was struck in realizing that we most often recognize the Way of Christ by the metaphorical footprints others leave in our daily lives. Clyde and I have worked together since 1999, and during these years his footprint has become increasingly clear in the way he touches others' lives.

Jesus was a carpenter, and he was walking through my front door.

The hospice's twenty-four hospice patient rooms line up, twelve to each side, down a long, well-lit hallway. The rooms are sunny and bright, warm and comfortable, and the light from their big windows spills into the hallway. Beside each doorway is the donor plaque for that room. The arched wooden backpieces of all are identical; the glasses and copper used for each are the same, with five different alternating designs. Across the face of each is a copper wire strung with moveable antique, handmade Christian, Hindu, Buddhist, Dead Sea salt, and Islamic prayer beads interspersed with engraved, patinated copper discs cut in squares, rectangles, and circles.

Beginning with the plaque of room 1 and walking room by room down the hall and making a loop back up the hall through room 24, the patient or family member, visitor or staff member, can read and move the words I engraved on the copper discs, words that are all included in the Hebrew and Christian Bibles and the Qur'an. The opening words of Psalm 23, "The Lord is my shepherd," are engraved on the first plaque, "I shall not want" on the second. After the end of Psalm 23, lines from Isaiah 43:1–7 begin: "Do not fear, for I have redeemed you; I have called you by name, you are mine."

Anyone who follows this path is walking—and is himself part of—a moving rosary, combining moving hands and feet with heart and mind in prayer.

Patients who come here know they cannot be cured physically, but many learn they can be healed, healed in spirit. In the care of staff trained in the art of dying, with the help of palliative medical care and the love of family educated about the needs at the end of life, they are made comfortable to deal with issues they and their families perhaps have been crippled by for years. People of all faiths, of no faith, of all socioeconomic levels are held in that holiest of places, a crucible between the Mystery of Life and the Mystery of Death and—as you and I eventually will, too—learn both that "in my beginning is my end" and "in my end is my beginning," which is also the path of a set of prayer beads.

And like those beads—stones as old as our universe—and the molten glass I work with, they and we—over unimaginable eons of tectonic and sedimentary change that are but a snap of the fingers in the crucibles of Time and Space—will ourselves become transformed into new matter, even possibly quarried and honed and held as future prayers in a future world, all shining like Merton's sun.

Acknowledgments

Ellen Morris Prewitt and Sybil MacBeth and other Vinton Writers Group foxhole buddies Blake Burr, Dan Stringfellow, Emma French Connolly, Joe Hawes, Kathy Hughes, Melinda Shoaf Kolb, Sandi Butler Hughes, Susan Cushman, Tom Carlson, and Frank Jemison, without whom this book would still be a dusty twenty pages; Rob Sanders, my first friend and first reader of my first-ever story; grandchildren Kate and Otto, for their drawings; Margaret Craddock, my fifteen-minutes-of-fame mentor; Jeff Nesin, for my turquoise iMac G3 and the exhortation "Go write!"; writer Richard Bausch and members of his Moss Writers Workshop semester; the encouragement of writer Bob Cowser and of woman-of-all-seasons Phyllis Tickle; Robbie McQuiston, for introducing me to Episcopal prayer beads; Jan Singer, for introducing me to fused glass; Mimsy Jones, for effortlessly conjuring up the book's title; Sharon Pavelda, for her hands and wardrobe of sweaters; Jeanne Jemison; second-mile heel-nipper Michelle Rich and others at Paraclete Press; the "pit crew of people," as Anne Lamott defines them, those friends without whom "life would be barren and prophetic . . . Death of a Salesman, though with email and texting"; and, of course, Jim Cole, the prince of my dotage.

Resources

Coles, Janet, and Robert Budwig. *Beads*. New York: Simons & Schuster, 1997.

_____. *The Book of Beads*. New York: Simon & Schuster, 1990.

Doerr, Nan Lewis, and Virginia Stem Owens. *Praying with Beads*. Grand Rapids, MI: Wm. B Eerdmans, 2007.

Hollis, James, PhD. *Finding Meaning in the Second Half of Life*. New York: Gotham Books, 2006.

Impastato, David, ed. *Upholding Mystery*. New York: Oxford University Press, 1997.

Lamott, Anne. *Help, Thanks, Wow*. New York: Riverhead Books, 2012.

Rohr, Richard. *Falling Upward*. San Francisco: Jossey-Bass, 2011.

_____. *Immortal Diamond*. San Francisco: Jossey-Bass, 2013.

Tickle, Phyllis. *The Divine Hours: Prayers for Summertime*. New York: Doubleday, 2000.

_____. *This Is What I Pray Today: The Divine Hours Prayers for Children*. New York: Penguin Group, 2007.

Vincent, Kristen E. *A Bead and a Prayer*. Nashville: Upper Room Books, 2013.

Vincent, Kristen E., and Max O. Vincent. *Another Bead, Another Prayer*. Nashville: Upper Room Books, 2014.

Wikstrom, Erik Walker. *Simply Pray*. Boston: Skinner House Books, 2005.

Wiley, Eleanor, and Maggie Oman Shannon. *A String and a Prayer*. York Beach, ME: Red Wheel/Weiser, 2002.

Winston, Kimberly. *Bead One, Pray Too*. New York: Morehouse Publishing, 2008.

HELPFUL WEBSITES:

www.abeadnaprayer.wordpress.com

www.ancientbead.com

www.iflscience.com/health-and-medicine/origins-human-heart-beat-traced-back-one-billion-years/

www.paternoster-row.com

www.prayerbedes.com

www.praxisofprayer.com

www.solitariesofdekoven.org

Notes

2   *To use beads with a prayer:* Madeleine L'Engle, *The Summer of the Great-Grandmother* (New York: HarperOne, 1984), 221.

14   *"circlet of gems":* John Desmond Miller, *Beads and Prayers: The Rosary in History and Devotion* (New York: Bloomsbury Publishing, 2002), 89.

25   *Always We Begin Again:* John McQuiston, II, *Always We Begin Again* (New York, Church Publishing, 1996).

31   *What is prayer?:* Elie Wiesel, Interview, *On Being with Krista Tippett,* July 8, 2016. https://onbeing.org/programs/evil-forgiveness-prayer-elie-wiesel/.

32   *"Prayer is a state of union,":* Interview, "Richard Rohr on Praying Like St. Francis," accessed December 19, 2017 *Franciscan Media* https://www.franciscanmedia.org/richard-rohr-on-praying-like-st-francis/.

36   *My Lord God,:* Thomas Merton, *Thoughts in Solitude* (New York: Dell, 1961).

44   *an ordinary moment:* Richard Rohr, "The Principle of Likeness: Smiling at Tide Boxes," Center for Action and Contemplation Daily Email, October 15, 2014.

45   *The Christian life:* Monica Furlong, *Travelling In* (London: Hodder and Stoughton, 1971), 98–99.

45   *In Louisville,:* Thomas Merton, *Conjectures of a Guilty Bystander* (New York: Image Books, 1968), 156.

49   *What is this Holy Spirit?:* David Craig, "Pentecost," in *Upholding Mystery,* ed. David Impastato (New York: Oxford University Press, 1997), 116.

65   *"just pretend you're good at it":* Jenny Lawson, *Pretend You're Good at It / The Bloggess,* February 9, 2016.

69   *"What the ego (False Self) hates:* Richard Rohr, *Immortal Diamond* (San Francisco: Jossey-Bass, 2013), 45.

82   *The problem with hell is:* Joseph Campbell, *Reflections on the Art of Living: A Joseph Campbell Companion,* selected and ed. Diane K. Osborn (Nashville, HarperCollins, 1991), 149, 151.

87   *"pit crew of people":* Anne Lamott, *Help, Thanks, Wow* (New York: Riverhead Books, 2012), 57.

About Paraclete Press

Who We Are

As the publishing arm of the Community of Jesus, Paraclete Press presents a full expression of Christian belief and practice—from Catholic to Evangelical, from Protestant to Orthodox, reflecting the ecumenical charism of the Community and its dedication to sacred music, the fine arts, and the written word. We publish books, recordings, sheet music, and DVDs that nourish the vibrant life of the church and its people.

What We Are Doing

BOOKS

PARACLETE PRESS BOOKS show the richness and depth of what it means to be Christian. While Benedictine spirituality is at the heart of who we are and all that we do, our books reflect the Christian experience across many cultures, time periods, and houses of worship.

We have many series, including *Paraclete Essentials; Paraclete Fiction; Paraclete Giants*; and the new *The Essentials of…*, devoted to Christian classics. Others include *Voices from the Monastery* (men and women monastics writing about living a spiritual life today), *Active Prayer*, the award-winning *Paraclete Poetry*, and new for young readers: *The Pope's Cat*. We also specialize in gift books for children on the occasions of Baptism and First Communion, as well as other important times in a child's life, and books that bring creativity and liveliness to any adult spiritual life.

The MOUNT TABOR BOOKS series focuses on the arts and literature as well as liturgical worship and spirituality; it was created in conjunction with the Mount Tabor Ecumenical Centre for Art and Spirituality in Barga, Italy.

MUSIC

The PARACLETE RECORDINGS label represents the internationally acclaimed choir *Gloriæ Dei Cantores*, the *Gloriæ Dei Cantores Schola*, and the other instrumental artists of the *Arts Empowering Life Foundation*.

Paraclete Press is the exclusive North American distributor for the Gregorian chant recordings from St. Peter's Abbey in Solesmes, France. Paraclete also carries all of the Solesmes chant publications for Mass and the Divine Office, as well as their academic research publications.

In addition, PARACLETE PRESS SHEET MUSIC publishes the work of today's finest composers of sacred choral music, annually reviewing over 1,000 works and releasing between 40 and 60 works for both choir and organ.

VIDEO

Our DVDs offer spiritual help, healing, and biblical guidance for a broad range of life issues including grief and loss, marriage, forgiveness, facing death, understanding suicide, bullying, addictions, Alzheimer's, and Christian formation.

Learn more about us at our website:
www.paracletepress.com or phone us toll-free at 1.800.451.5006

SCAN
TO
READ
MORE

You may also be interested in …

Praying in Color
Drawing a New Path to God
SYBIL MACBETH
ISBN: 978-1-55725-512-9, $17.99

Writing to God
40 Days of Praying with My Pen
RACHEL HACKENBERG
ISBN: 978-1-55725-879-3, $15.99

Making Crosses
A Creative Connection to God
ELLEN MORRIS PREWITT
ISBN: 978-1-55725-628-7, $18.99

Praying with the Body
Bringing the Psalms to Life
ROY DELEON
ISBN: 978-1-55725-589-1, $18.99

Available from most booksellers or through Paraclete Press:
www.paracletepress.com | 1-800-451-5006
Try your local bookstore first.